First World War
and Army of Occupation
War Diary
France, Belgium and Germany

39 DIVISION
Divisional Troops
174 and 179 Brigade Royal Field Artillery
19 May 1915 - 18 January 1917

WO95/2574/3

The Naval & Military Press Ltd
www.nmarchive.com
Published in association with The National Archives

Published by

The Naval & Military Press Ltd

Unit 10 Ridgewood Industrial Park,

Uckfield, East Sussex,

TN22 5QE England

Tel: +44 (0) 1825 749494

www.naval-military-press.com

www.nmarchive.com

This diary has been reprinted in facsimile from the original. Any imperfections are inevitably reproduced and the quality may fall short of modern type and cartographic standards.

© **Crown Copyright**
Images reproduced by permission of The National Archives, London, England, 2015.

Contents

Document type	Place/Title	Date From	Date To
Heading	WO95/2574 Nov 16-Dec 18 174 Bde R.F.A. (Missing July/Dec 1917 Inclusive)		
Heading	39th Division Divl Artillery 174th Brigade R.F.A. Mar 1916-Dec 1918 July-Dec 1917 Lac Missing		
Heading	39th Divisional Artillery. Formed 19th May 1915. Disembarked Havre 4.3.16		
Miscellaneous	174 R.F.A. Vol 1		
War Diary	Deptford	19/05/1915	31/09/1915
War Diary	Ewshott	02/10/1915	12/10/1915
War Diary	Twezeldown	13/10/1915	29/11/1915
War Diary	Milford	04/12/1915	30/01/1916
War Diary	Lark Hill	01/02/1916	06/02/1916
War Diary	Milford	14/02/1916	03/03/1916
War Diary	Southampton	03/03/1916	03/03/1916
War Diary	Le Havre	04/03/1916	06/03/1916
War Diary	Lynde	09/03/1916	09/03/1916
War Diary	Neuf Berguin	11/03/1916	11/03/1916
War Diary	Laventie	13/03/1916	25/03/1916
War Diary	Mazinghem	26/03/1916	31/03/1916
Heading	39th Divisional Artillery. "D" Battery 174th Brigade R.F.A. March 1916		
Miscellaneous	D' 174 RFA Vol 1		
War Diary	Milford.	03/03/1916	03/03/1916
War Diary	Southampton	03/03/1916	03/03/1916
War Diary	Hovre	04/03/1916	05/03/1916
War Diary	In The Train	06/03/1916	07/03/1916
War Diary	Blaringham	08/03/1916	10/03/1916
War Diary	Machin	11/03/1916	23/03/1916
War Diary	Bac St Maur	24/03/1916	25/03/1916
War Diary	Molinghem	26/03/1916	31/03/1916
Heading	39th Divisional Artillery. 174th Brigade Royal Field Artillery. April 1916		
War Diary	Mazinghem	02/04/1916	15/04/1916
War Diary	Gorre	15/04/1916	25/04/1916
War Diary	Givency.	26/04/1916	30/04/1916
Heading	39th Divisional Artillery. 174th Brigade Royal Field Artillery. May 1916		
War Diary	Givency.	01/05/1916	12/05/1916
War Diary	Locon	13/05/1916	25/05/1916
War Diary	Givenchy	25/05/1916	31/05/1916
Heading	39th Divisional Artillery. 174th Brigade Royal Field Artillery. June 1916		
War Diary	Givenchy	01/06/1916	19/06/1916
War Diary	Richebourg	19/06/1916	01/07/1916
Heading	39th Divisional Artillery. 174th Brigade Royal Field Artillery July 1916		
Miscellaneous	To H.Q. 39th Div Arty	31/07/1916	31/07/1916
War Diary	Richebourg	01/07/1916	27/07/1916
War Diary	In The Field	27/07/1916	31/07/1916

Heading	39th Divisional Artillery. 174th Brigade. Royal Field Artillery. August 1916		
War Diary	Bethune	01/08/1916	07/08/1916
War Diary	Movins	09/08/1916	25/08/1916
War Diary	Mailly Engelbelmer On R. Ancre	25/08/1916	26/08/1916
War Diary	Mailly	26/08/1916	31/08/1916
Heading	39th Divisional Artillery. 174th Brigade Royal Field Artillery. September 1916		
Heading	War Diary Of 174th Brigade Royal Field Artillery From 1st September 1916 To 30th September 1916		
War Diary	Mailly	01/09/1916	30/09/1916
Heading	39th Divisional Artillery. 174th Brigade Royal Field Artillery. October 1916		
War Diary	Q25d9.3.	01/10/1916	31/10/1916
Heading	12th Bde. 4th Division. War Diary 2nd Lancashire Fusiliers 1915		
Heading	39th Divisional Artillery. 174th Brigade Royal Field Artillery. November 1916		
Heading	174 Brigade R.F.A. War Diary Sheet 22-23 For Period 1/11/16-30/11/16		
War Diary	Q25d.9.3.	01/11/1916	18/11/1916
War Diary	Hamel	19/11/1916	30/11/1916
Heading	39th Divisional Artillery. 174th Brigade Royal Field Artillery. December 1916		
Heading	War Diary 174th Brigade R.F.A. Sheet 24 1/12/16 To 31/12/16		
War Diary	Arneke	01/12/1916	14/12/1916
War Diary	Ypres Salient. (Left).	15/12/1916	31/12/1916
Heading	War Diary 174th Brigade Royal Field Artillery Sheet 24 Jan 1st 1917 To Jan 31rd 1917		
War Diary	Ypes Salient Left	01/01/1917	03/01/1917
War Diary	Hq. Regersbert	05/01/1917	17/01/1917
War Diary	I8d.1.9.	18/01/1917	31/01/1917
War Diary	Ypres.	01/02/1917	31/03/1917
War Diary	Lille Gate	01/04/1917	01/04/1917
War Diary	Ypres	02/04/1917	09/04/1917
War Diary	Houtkerque & Wateu	10/04/1917	17/04/1917
War Diary	Lederzeele Lecques.	18/04/1917	19/04/1917
War Diary	Wissant	20/04/1917	30/04/1917
War Diary	Wissant	01/05/1917	02/05/1917
War Diary	Licques	03/05/1917	03/05/1917
War Diary	Lederzeele	04/05/1917	04/05/1917
War Diary	Watou	05/05/1917	31/05/1917
War Diary	Peselhoek	01/06/1917	30/06/1917
War Diary		01/01/1918	28/02/1918
Heading	39th Div. War Dairy Headquarters, 174th Brigade, R.F.A. March 1918		
War Diary		01/03/1918	31/03/1918
Heading	39th Divisional Artillery. 174th Brigade R.F.A. April 1918.		
War Diary		01/04/1918	30/06/1918
Operation(al) Order(s)	Right Group Operation Order No.2 Appendix "A"	31/05/1918	31/05/1918
Miscellaneous	Right Group-57th D.A. Operation Order No. 6	26/06/1918	26/06/1918
War Diary		01/07/1918	31/08/1918
War Diary	Nr Cherisy.	01/09/1918	30/09/1918
War Diary		01/10/1918	31/12/1918

Heading	WO95/2574 Nov. 16-Jan 17 179 Bde RFA		
Heading	39th Division Divl Artillery 179th Brigade R.F.A. Mar 1916-Jan 1917 To 5 Army		
Heading	39th Divisional Artillery. Disembarked Havre 5th March 1916 179th Brigade Royal Field Artillery. March 1916 Jan 1917		
Heading	War Diary Of 179th Bde. R.F.A. From March 4th 1916 To March 31st 1916 (Volume 1)		
War Diary	Milford Sumey	04/03/1916	04/03/1916
War Diary	France	05/03/1916	05/03/1916
War Diary	Havre	06/03/1916	06/03/1916
War Diary	Blaringhem	07/03/1916	10/03/1916
War Diary	Estaires	11/03/1916	11/03/1916
War Diary	Fleurbaix	12/03/1916	25/03/1916
War Diary	Berguette	26/03/1916	31/03/1916
Heading	39th Divisional Artillery 179th Brigade Royal Field Artillery April 1916		
War Diary	Berguette	01/04/1916	15/04/1916
War Diary	Loisnes	16/04/1916	30/04/1916
Miscellaneous	39th Divisional Artillery. Operation Order No 3.		
Heading	39th Divisional Artillery. 179th Brigade Royal Field Artillery. May 1916		
War Diary	Loisnes	01/05/1916	18/05/1916
War Diary	Locon	23/05/1916	31/05/1916
Heading	39th Divisional Artillery. 179th Brigade Royal Field Artillery. June 1916		
War Diary	Locon	01/05/1916	30/05/1916
Heading	39th Divisional Artillery. 179th Brigade Royal Field Artillery. July 1916		
Miscellaneous	HQ 39th R.A.	31/07/1916	31/07/1916
War Diary	Locon	01/07/1916	06/07/1916
War Diary	Tourbieres	07/07/1916	14/07/1916
War Diary	Lacouture	15/07/1916	26/07/1916
War Diary	Loisnes	27/07/1916	31/07/1916
Operation(al) Order(s)	Operation Order No. 3		
Operation(al) Order(s)	Operation Order No. 5		
Miscellaneous	C Group. R.F.A. Operation Order No 12		
Heading	39th Divisional Artillery. 179th Brigade Royal Field Artillery. August 1916		
War Diary	Loisnes	01/08/1916	10/08/1916
War Diary	Lieres	11/08/1916	11/08/1916
War Diary	Roellcourt	12/08/1916	20/08/1916
War Diary	Lucheux	21/08/1916	21/08/1916
War Diary	Thievres	22/08/1916	25/08/1916
War Diary	Bus. Les-Artois.	26/08/1916	31/08/1916
Heading	War Diary 179th Bde R.F.A. Volume I Month Of August 1916		
Heading	39th Divisional Artillery. 179th Brigade Royal Field Artillery September 1916		
War Diary	Bus-Les-Artois	01/09/1916	04/09/1916
War Diary	Mailly. Maillet	05/09/1916	20/09/1916
War Diary	P.6.a.4.3.	21/09/1916	22/09/1916
War Diary	Beussart	23/09/1916	30/09/1916
Operation(al) Order(s)	Group Operation Order No. 2		
Heading	39th Divisional Artillery. 179th Brigade Royal Field Artillery October 1916		

War Diary	Beausart	01/10/1916	02/10/1916
War Diary	Vitermont	03/10/1916	17/10/1916
War Diary	Englebelmer	18/10/1916	31/10/1916
Heading	39th Divisional Artillery. 179th Brigade Royal Field Artillery. November 1916		
War Diary	Englebelmer	01/11/1916	27/11/1916
War Diary	Arneke	28/11/1916	30/11/1916
Heading	39th Divisional Artillery. 179th Brigade Royal Field Artillery. December 1916		
War Diary	Arneke	01/12/1916	06/12/1916
War Diary	Watou	07/12/1916	08/12/1916
War Diary	Elverdinghe	09/12/1916	18/01/1917

WO95/2574
Mar '16 – Dec '18
174 Bde RFA.

(Missing July/Dec 1917 inclusive)

39TH DIVISION
DIVL ARTILLERY

174TH BRIGADE R.F.A.

MAR 1916-DEC 1918

July - Dec 1917 inc.
missing

39th Divisional Artillery.

Formed 19th May 1915: Disembarked HAVRE 4.3.16.

174th BRIGADE

ROYAL FIELD ARTILLERY

19.5.15 to 31st MARCH 1916.

Dec '18

174 R.7A
Vol 1

Army Form C. 2118

WAR DIARY INTELLIGENCE SUMMARY

(Erase heading not required.)

174th Brigade, R. F. A.

Instructions regarding War Diaries and Intelligence Summaries are contained in F.S. Regs., Part II. and the Staff Manual respectively. Title Pages will be prepared in manuscript.

Place	Date	Hour	Summary of Events and Information	Remarks and references to Appendices
Deptford	19/5/15		The authority for the formation of the 174th Brigade, R.F.A. (Deptford) is contained in War Office letter No. 20/General No/3847 (A.G.1) dated 19th 1915. May	
			Authority was requested by the Mayor of Deptford, W.A. Wayland, Esq., M.P. to form a local Brigade of Artillery. Various recruiting meetings were held, and recruits came forward in large numbers with the excellent result that the 174th Brigade was formed in the record time of 6½ days. After which the recruits over establishment were drafted to the second Deptford Brigade, the 179th Brigade, R.F.A.	
27. 5.15	Deptford		The first parade of recruits was at Deptford Town Hall on the morning of 27th May 1915, when headed by the Central London Recruiting Band the men were marched to Headquarters at Penn's Iron Works, Blackheath Road, S.E.	
Deptford	7/6/15		Major E.R.Phillips, R.F.A. assumed Command of the Brigade.	
"	10/6/15		Lieut. W.F.H. Rowe having joined the Brigade was appointed Adjutant on 10th June 1915.	
"			The recruits paraded daily for instruction on Blackheath in Squad Drill, etc.	
"	14/6/15		A recruiting parade was held in Deptford Broadway, at which the Mayor of Deptford and several local gentlemen spoke.	
"	10/6/15		Clothing was first issued on June 10th 1915, and finished about 16th June.	
"	7/6/15		2 Lieut. D.G.S. Gregory joined the Brigade.	
"	19/6/15		2 " A.M. Diamant joined the Brigade.	
"	23/6/15		A smoking concert was given at Goldsmith's College Lewisham High Road, S.E. at which the Mayor of Deptford presided.	
"	23/6/15		2 Lieut. L.S. Edmonds joined the Brigade 2 " C.G. Vandyk joined the Brigade.	

Army Form C. 2118

174th Brigade, R.F.A.

WAR DIARY ~~INTELLIGENCE SUMMARY~~
(Erase heading not required.)

Instructions regarding War Diaries and Intelligence Summaries are contained in F.S. Regs., Part II. and the Staff Manual respectively. Title Pages will be prepared in manuscript.

Place	Date	Hour	Summary of Events and Information	Remarks and references to Appendices
Deptford	June 24		- 2 - continued.	
			The Brigade was inspected by General Sir Francis Lloyd on Blackheath.	
"	" 25		2 Lieut. S.I. Quin, joined the Brigade.	
"	" 28		2 " H.L. Fitsell joined the Brigade.	
"	" 28		2 " W.F. Mead joined the Brigade.	
"	July 5		The first horses were posted to the Brigade on July 5th 1915, and these were stabled in Penn's Iron Works	
"	" 5		2 Lieutenant S.E.C. Lamb joined the Brigade.	
"	" 12		2 " R.C. Webb joined the Brigade.	
"	" 19		The horses of the Brigade were inspected by the A.D.V.S. London District, and a great many cases of ring-worm were reported.	
"	" 20		The D.A.D.R. London District inspected the Horses of the Brigade.	
"	" 28		2 Lieutenant T.C. Griffin joined the Brigade from France.	
"	Aug. 3		A Ceremonial parade was held on this date on the anniversary of the Declaration of war by England on Germany. The wagons and teams were paraded for the first time on ceremonial parade.	
"	" 6		2 Lieut. H.C.F. Butcher joined the Brigade.	
"	" 10		2 " M.R. Pitman joined the Brigade.	
			Lieut. E.J. Fox joined the Brigade.	
"	" 12		Four wooden guns were posted to the Brigade for instructional purposes.	

E.R. Phillips
Lieut-Col R.F.A.
174th Bde R.F.A.

Army Form C. 2118

WAR DIARY / INTELLIGENCE SUMMARY

(Erase heading not required.)

174th Brigade, R.F.A.

Instructions regarding War Diaries and Intelligence Summaries are contained in F.S. Regs., Part II. and the Staff Manual respectively. Title Pages will be prepared in manuscript.

Place	Date	Hour	Summary of Events and Information	Remarks and references to Appendices
Deptford	23 Aug		2 Lieut. A.G. Whitehouse joined the Brigade.	
"	24 "		The first guns were allotted to the Brigade on this date (two in number) 18 pr.Q.F.	
"	28 "		A cricket match was played at Goldsmiths College Grounds between Deptford Town Hall Staff and the Deptford Gun Brigades.	
"	Sep. 4		2 Lieut. H.A. Pay joined the Brigade.	
"	" 11		All members of the Deptford Brigades were invited to a cricket match at Kennington Oval, when a great recruiting rally was held.	
"	" 14		2 Lieut. T.C. Griffin was appointed Adjutant of the Brigade.	
"	" 19		A Drum Head Service was held on Hilly Fields, Brockley on Sunday morning 19.9.15.	
"	" 20		A photo of all the Officers of the Brigade was taken at Goldsmiths College, Lewisham.	
"	" 22		A photo of the whole of the Brigade was taken on the Upper parade ground at Penn's Iron Works.	
"	" 22		2 Lieut. E.S. Wise joined the Brigade.	
"	" 23		A ceremonial parade was held on this date, each Battery and Ammunition Column sending eight teams.	
"	" 23		The Advance party of the Brigade left New Cross Station for Aldershot Station in preparation of the Brigade moving to 49, Camp, Ewshott, Aldershot. 2 Lieuts. Lamb, Butcher and 40 N.C.O.'s and men comprised this party.	
"	" 31		The Brigade entrained at Arsenal Station for Aldershot Town Station. The first party left during the afternoon of the 31st August September, and the last in the early morning of 1st October 1915, the last party arriving at 49, Camp, Ewshott at about 10 a.m.	

J.M. Phillips
Lieut-Col R.A.
Commdg. 174th Bde R.F.A.

Army Form C. 2118

WAR DIARY
or
INTELLIGENCE SUMMARY
(Erase heading not required.)

174th Brigade, R.F.A.

Instructions regarding War Diaries and Intelligence Summaries are contained in F.S. Regs., Part II. and the Staff Manual respectively. Title Pages will be prepared in manuscript.

Place	Date	Hour	Summary of Events and Information	Remarks and references to Appendices
Ewshott	Oct. 2		Capt A.P. Ford joined the Brigade as Medical Officer.	
"	" 2		2 Lieut. T.E. Sierra joined the Brigade.	
"	" 2		2 " O.B.H. Delamaine) joined the Brigade.	
"	" 5		Inspection by G.O.C. A.C. on Long Valley in Field Service Marching Order.	
"	" 6		2 Lieut. O.W. Care joined the Brigade.	
"	" 6		2 " E.V. Johnson joined the Brigade.	
"	" 12		The Brigade moved from 49 Camp, Ewshott to Haig Hutments, Twezeldown, Farnham.	
Twezeldown	" 13		2 Lieut. E.H. Knowles joined the Brigade.	
"	" 19		The Brigade was inspected by the G.O.C. R.A. on Long Valley in Drill Order. each Battery turned out 12 teams.	
"	" 15		87166 Battery Quartermaster Sergeant T. Mahon appointed Regimental Sergeant Major.	
"	" 11		Inoculation Commenced.	

E.P. Phillips
Lieut Col. R.F.A
Commdg. 174th Bde R.F.A

Army Form C. 2118.

WAR DIARY
or
INTELLIGENCE SUMMARY.   174th Brigade R.F.A.

(Erase heading not required.)

Instructions regarding War Diaries and Intelligence Summaries are contained in F.S. Regs., Part II and the Staff Manual respectively. Title pages will be prepared in manuscript.

Place	Hour, Date	Summary of Events and Information	Remarks and references to Appendices
Tweseldown	October 15th	Lecture by an M.P. on "Munition Work" at Evshott	
=	15th	2 Lieut. E.H. Knowles joined the Brigade.	
=	20th	Inspection by G.O.C. 39th Division, on Long Valley, in Field Service Marching Order	
=	=	Captain J.A.I. French joined the Brigade	
	November 4th	Divisional Artillery Tactical Exercise.	
=	6	Advance party leaves Tweseldown, for new station at Milford Camp Surrey	
=	8	The Brigade moved to New Station at Milford Camp, by road, leaving Tweseldown	
=		at 9. a.m.	
=	22	2 Lieut. R.H. Griffin joined the Brigade.	
	6	2 Lieut. H.C. Hooker. joined the Brigade	
	29	Boxing Tournament in Dining Hall of the 174th Brigade R.F.A. President,	
		Lieut. T.C. Griffin. R.F.A.	

W. Gillie
Lieut - col. RFA
Comdg. 174th Bde RFA.

(73989) W4141—463. 400,000. 9/14. H.&J.Ltd. Forms/C. 2118/10.

WAR DIARY
or
INTELLIGENCE SUMMARY

Army Form C. 2118

Instructions regarding War Diaries and Intelligence Summaries are contained in F.S. Regs., Part II. and the Staff Manual respectively. Title Pages will be prepared in manuscript.

(Erase heading not required.)

Place	Date	Hour	Summary of Events and Information	Remarks and references to Appendices
Milford	Dec 4	—	Six days Christmas Leave commenced – completed January 8th.	
"	" 23	7 pm.	Concert given to the Brigade by selection of Artists.	
"	Jan 1.		Declared a General Holiday to all Brigades of 39th Division.	
"	" 30		Brigade moved to No 22 Canada Lines, Lark Hill Aldershot, for two weeks course.	
Lark Hill	Feb 1		Gunnery Course, camp within sight of "Stonehenge".	
"	" 6		First shot fired by A Battery. – Gypsification commenced.	
"			Left Lark Hill this day for Milford.	
Milford	" 14		Half of Brigade left for two days Musketry Course at Ash Range No 2, Aldershot	
"	" 16		2nd half of Brigade left for two days Musketry Course at Ash Range No 4 "	
"	" 16		Half of Brigade left on 4 days final leave prior to move overseas. do	
"	" 28		2nd half of Brigade left on 4 days do do do	
"	Mar 3.		First Party of Bde left for overseas. Arrived at Southampton 5 pm. Embarkation of Bde Headquarters & Batteries at. commenced.	
Southampton	" 3		Ship "South Western Miller" left quayside at 7.30 pm.	
"	" 3		Ship hove to in bay during early hours of morning. Disembarkation Commenced at 12 noon	
Le Havre	" 4		Entrained at Halle 3, Gare du hord, at 11.15 pm.	
"	" 4		Arrived at Steenbecque at 3.30 pm & proceeded to farmhouse close to Lynde. Batteries billetted in farmhouses around.	
"	" 6			

E.G.Phillips Lieut. Col. R.A.
Comdg. 174th Bde R.F.A.

WAR DIARY
or
INTELLIGENCE SUMMARY

(Erase heading not required.)

Army Form C. 2118

Place	Date	Hour	Summary of Events and Information	Remarks and references to Appendices
Lynde	9/3/16	8.30 a.m	The Brigade left Lynde at 8.30 a.m. and proceeded to ESTAIRES, by road, arriving there at 5.30pm	
NEUF. BERGUIN	11/3/16	6.15pm	Same day, Headquarters billetted in a farmhouse at NEUF BERGUIN and Batteries and Ammn Cn. in farmhouses in the vicinity. Brigade proceeded to Laventie, arriving at 8.15 pm (with the exception of the B.A.C. which moved to ESTAIRES.) The Headquarters Batteries & various farmhouses Mar.e. The Batteries took over firing positions as follows. A Battery — M. 21. b.8.7. B " — N.10. c.8.5 C " — N.3. C.4.4 " — M.34. a.4.4 attached 8th Division 3rd Corps	Red horse Sect 26 Belgium part of France ① Trench map No 1 Edition 6 1/10,000
LAVENTIE	12/3/16		M.11.C.4.5. 13.3.16. 3pm. LE CLERQ FARM N.27. b.7½. 8½. 7 rounds shrapnel. Registration 2.45 pm DE RAPORTE FARM N.15.a. 7.5. 2 " " " " 3.10 pm QUESTION HOUSE N.14 b. 5. 1½. 3 " " " " 3.20 pm JUSA'S HOUSE N.14. d. 9½. 7 5 " " " " 3.30 pm ORCHARD HOUSE N.14.b. 8. 2½. 4 " " " " 3.40 pm ISEACH. JUNCTION N.16.b. 1. 3½. 3 " " " " German observation balloon seen 3.30pm. from N.13.a.9.8. Bearing from true north 112.30. R.	
LAVENTIE	13/3/16		D Battery. Point in German Trench opposite N.81. Registered 3 rounds fired at ·53, with excellent results to judge from the appearance of the burst.	
LAVENTIE	14.3.16		Hostile Artillery "Papaquenhas" + 5.9o reported from LE PLOUICH M.28.a.1.3. shelled "C" Battery's position at M, 11.C.5.5. About 200 shells from 9.30am to 10.50 am.	
-do-	15.3.16		During afternoon enemy 4.2 howitzer threw a light shell on to tramway stone, close to D.Battery. No firing by Brigade today.	

E.C.Phillips
Lieut.Col. R.F.A.
Comdg. 174th Brigade, R.F.A.

WAR DIARY or INTELLIGENCE SUMMARY

(Erase heading not required.)

Instructions regarding War Diaries and Intelligence Summaries are contained in F.S. Regs., Part II. and the Staff Manual respectively. Title Pages will be prepared in manuscript.

Place	Date	Hour	Summary of Events and Information	Remarks and references to Appendices
LAVENTIE	16/3/16	10.30am	Enemy Artillery shelled "C" Battery M.11.c.7.2. at 10.30am about 6 rounds.	
		2 pm	" " " "C" " " " about 2 rounds.	
		2-3 pm	" " " D Battery N.28.c.3.3. — 50 rounds 4.2. Position of Observer H.34.A.4.4.	
		4.30 pm	" " " Bde Headquarters + wagon lines, about 20 rounds 77 mm gun shrapnel	
LAVENTIE	17.3.16.	3.30pm	A Battery. 10 shrapnel fired at Point 85 — Registered zero line.	
		2.30 pm	B. " registered 5 rounds on N.19.c.3½.4½.	
			" " 4 rounds on LES MOTTES FERME.	
		4 pm	C " 12 rounds on N.14.b.6.0. — on screen hiding road — satisfactory.	
		2 pm	D " 3 rounds on Pt. 53.	
			" " 3 " S. " N.14.b.½.5.	
			" " 6 " S. " N.13.d.4.4.	
LAVENTIE	18.3.16	—	A Battery reported that enemy shelled 13.A.c.6.63 — 6 H.E. large. Sound bearing 4° left of AUBERS CHIMNEY from 13.A.c.5.6.	
		2.45pm	C " reported that enemy shelled N.7.d.2½. with 4.2 gun.	
		9 — 9.30am	D " " " " N.28.c.3.3 with 4.2 gun — 10 rounds fired	
		2-2.30am	D " " " " N.28.c.3.3 with 4.2 gun — 25 rounds fired	
		6pm	A Battery registered 6 rounds on zero line, 1st night line.	
		8.20pm	A " " 5 " S. on N.19.e.3.2½.	
		3.50pm	B " " 3 " S. on N.19.c.5.0	

E.R. Phillips
Lieut. & Adjt. R.F.A.
Comdg. 174th Bde. R.F.A.

WAR DIARY or INTELLIGENCE SUMMARY

(Erase heading not required.)

Instructions regarding War Diaries and Intelligence Summaries are contained in F. S. Regs., Part II. and the Staff Manual respectively. Title Pages. will be prepared in manuscript.

Place	Date	Hour	Summary of Events and Information	Remarks and references to Appendices
LAVENTIE	19/3/16	3.30pm	A Battery fired 8 shrapnel on N.13.D.3.7 Range 3500-3600.	
"		3 pm	A " " 2 " " N.20.B.3.5	
"		3 pm	B " " 6 " on N.19.c.3.7 + N.19.c.3-8½	
"		4 pm	C " " 12 " on N.21.b2.4½	
"		3.30pm	D " " 5 " on N.13.C.9.2 - Registered	
"	20.3.16	2.45pm	A Battery fired 4 rounds shrapnel on N.20.a.7.8½.	
"		4.30pm	C " " 9 " " N.14.B.3.4.	
"		3.30pm to 4.30pm	D " " 3 " " N.14.C.2.3.} Ends of German Tramways.	
"			" " 2 " " N.14.C.5.3.}	
"			" " 7 " " N.14.C.7.6 Germans working in Trenches.	
"	21/3/16	11.55 am	Enemy Artillery 77mm battery fired one blind shell at point M.21.b.7.3½ from M.21.b.8.7. bearing 122°30'.	
"		3.30pm	B Battery fired 4 rounds shrapnel on N.25.b.5.2½.	
"			" " 3 " H.E. on N.25.b.5.2½.—one direct hit.	
"	22.3.16		— nil reports.	

R.G. Phillips
Lieut. Col. R.F.A.
Comdg. 174th Bde R.F.A.

INTELLIGENCE SUMMARY

Instructions regarding War Diaries and Intelligence Summaries are contained in F.S. Regs, Part II. and the Staff Manual respectively. Title Pages will be prepared in manuscript.

(Erase heading not required.)

Place	Date	Hour	Summary of Events and Information	Remarks and references to Appendices
LAVENTIE	23/3/16		NIL REPORTS.	
"	24/3/16		2 Lieut N.E. Stutchfield joined Brigade, + was attached to A Battery. 2 " N.B. Heath " " " B.Battery. NIL REPORTS on our own + enemy's artillery. Batteries withdrew from Gun positions to wagon lines.	
"	25/3/16	8.15 am	Brigade (less ~~~~) left Laventie for Mazingham, arriving at 6.30 pm Route — ESTAIRES — Pt LEVIS (L.24). Road Junction — K.30-d.7.8. — MERVILLE — ROBECQ Batteries + Amn Column billeted in the vicinity. Attached 33rd Division, 11th Corps.	Ref Map these Sheet 36 a. 1/40,000
MAZINGHEM	26/3/16 to 31/3/16		Resting in Reserve in billets around MAZINGHEM.	

EPhillips

39th Divisional Artillery.

"D" BATTERY

174th BRIGADE R.F.A.

MARCH 1916

Army Form C. 2118

D 174 R.F.A
Vol 1

Army Form C. 2118

WAR DIARY
INTELLIGENCE SUMMARY
(Erase heading not required.)

D. Battery – 174. Bde. –
Page. 1

Instructions regarding War Diaries and Intelligence Summaries are contained in F.S. Regs., Part II. and the Staff Manual respectively. Title Pages will be prepared in manuscript.

Place	Date	Hour	Summary of Events and Information	Remarks and references to Appendices
Milford	March 3rd	12 noon	Right half Battery leaves Milford by train for SOUTHAMPTON.	
		1 p.m.	" " left " " " " " "	
Southampton		8 p.m.	The Battery leaves dock on the 'South Western Miller'. The whole Bde, less the Amm. Colm on board.	
Havre	4th	10 A.m.	Dis-embark at HAVRE + march for the night to No. 2. Rest-Camp arriving there at 8. p.m. – Unité Canvas –	
Havre	5th	11.30 p.m.	The Battery entrains, leaving the GARE des MARCHANDISES at 11.30 p.m. –	
In train	6th	5. a.m.	Water + feed at MONTPELLIER.	
		11 a.m.	do do ABBEVILLE.	
		6. p.m.	Detrain at STEENBECQUE + march into billets between BLARINGHEM	
	7th		and SERCUS – arriving at 1.30 A.m. Snow thick on the ground –	
Blaringhem	8th		In billets –	

Army Form C. 2118

WAR DIARY
or
INTELLIGENCE SUMMARY

D Battery - 174 Bde. R.F.A.
Page 2.

(Erase heading not required.)

Place	Date	Hour	Summary of Events and Information	Remarks and references to Appendices
Blaringham	9th	9 A.m.	Leave billets after a very hard frost & march into new billets between ESTAIRES & NEUF BERQUIN.	
	10th	5 p.m.	Reconnoitre the Battery's position in the morning. The Right Section go up into action at CROIX MARECHAL - H.34.a.4.4. A good position enfilading the German trenches. Attached to the 5th Batt 8th Divn. for instruction.	
In action.	11th		In action. Much work put into the pits. Lovely weather.	
	12th			
	13th		A little quiet registering. The Left Section detachments come up to the pits. (15th)	
	14th /to 18th			
	19th /to 22		Weather generally dull - a little firing.	
	23rd	7 p.m.	Move down to wagon line at FORT ROMPUE near BAC ST MAUR.	

Army Form C. 2118

WAR DIARY
or
INTELLIGENCE SUMMARY   D. Battery, 174 Bde R.F.A.
Page 3

(Erase heading not required.)

Place	Date	Hour	Summary of Events and Information	Remarks and references to Appendices
BAC ST MAUR	24th		In wagon line all day. Snowing.	
	25th		March into billets near MOLINGHEM (AIRE) arriving at 6.45 p.m.	
MOLINGHEM	26th		2/Lt J.E. Siena joins the Battery to join the French Mortar School at St. VENANT. Brig. Gen. G. Gilam D.S.O. takes over the command of the Divil Artillery.	
	27th		2/Lt M.B. Heath joins the Battery.	
	28th – 31st		In billets. Canteen opened, in conjunction with the Bde. Amn Coln on the 30th.	

39th Divisional Artillery.

174th BRIGADE

ROYAL FIELD ARTILLERY.

APRIL 1916

WAR DIARY
INTELLIGENCE SUMMARY

Army Form C. 2118.

174 RFA Vol 2

Place	Date	Hour	Summary of Events and Information	Remarks and references to Appendices
MAZINGHEM	9/4/16		Personnel as under attached to 33rd Divl Artillery for Instruction in CUINCHY Section.	
			A. Battery 2 Officers 20 Other Ranks to A/166 Bty.	
			B " 2 " 20 " " C "	
			C " 2 " 20 " " B "	
			D " 2 " 20 " " D/162 "	
	10/4/16		Similar party, as details above, were attached to 33rd Divl Artillery in relief of personnel attached on 9 inst.	
	11/4/16		Lieut Colonel J.G.R. Allardyce R.Z.A assumes Command of the Brigade. Vice Colonel C.R. Phillips R.F.A. from 1st B.R.F.A.	
	12/4/16		(to England) Au7. 1st Army Order no 115/703A dated 7/4/16. 2/Lt S.R. Barham R.Z.a Joins for duty, with B Battery.	
	13/4/16		Operation Order No 7. Brigade from 39 Div A.I. — 39 Divl Arty to relieve 33rd Divl Arty (and attached Battery [A/156]) 33rd Division on 14/15 April.	
	14/4/16		A/174 } 1 Section Left MAZINGHEM at 3.30 A.M. and proceeded to :- A Battery. X.8.d.1.9 (wagon lines) & the following	Ref map "40000" BETHUNE Combined Sheet :-
			B } roads. B " X.9.c.4.6. "	{ 36 A S.E.
			C } C " X.13.d.2.3. "	36 B N.E.
			D } D " X.19.b.7.5. "	36 C S.W.
			Route :- HAM-EN-ARTOIS — BUSNES — ROBECQ. HINGES. — AVELETTE — and thence & wagon lines, taking up Gun Position Batteries detailed below.	36 C N.W.
			TIME OF ARRIVAL UNIT RELIEVED GUN POSITION	
			A/174 } A/120 X.22.d.6.6.	
			B } Relief completed B/120 X.24.c.6.9.	
			C } by 7pm C/120 } S.14.c.1.7.	
			D } A/156 } A.13.b.5.4.	
			D/120	

Jacon?
Lt Colonel R.F.A.
Cmdg 174 Brigade R.F.A.

30.4.16.

Sheet 13. Army Form C. 2118.

WAR DIARY or INTELLIGENCE SUMMARY.
(Erase heading not required.)

Place	Date	Hour	Summary of Events and Information	Remarks and references to Appendices
MAZINGHEM	15/4/16.		The undermentioned moves has been carried out. Starting time 2.30 am. Hd Qts & batteries 3.30 am. B.A.C. 5.30 am.	

UNIT	FROM	TO WAGON LINES	ROUTE	TIME of ARRIVAL	UNIT RELIEVED	GUN POSITION	
Hd Qtrs	MAZINGHEM	F.10.b.5.2.	As on 14 inst.	Move completed by 7pm	B. Group H.Q. (121st Bde RFA)	MAP REF: 2 hours on 14" + 15" are at Sheet 40000 36A	+ Combined BETHUNE Sheet.
A) 1	"	"			As on 14"	As on 14"	Also Trench Map N.W. No 1.
B) SECTION	"	"					
C) EACH	"	"					10000 Ed. 6.
D)	"	"					
B.A.C.	"	W.22.d.9.5.			B.A.C. 120/Bde.		

GORRE — Headquarters 174 Bde R.F.A. became "B" Group Headquarters. Lt. Col 79B Allaoqu. Commanding the Group. Composed of the following Units:

B/174. Battery R.F.A. A/186 Battery R.F.A. 4.5" How (6 Hours)
D/174. ½ B/186. }
A/184
B/186 + ½ C/184   } 15pr. B.L. (20 guns)
½ C/184 (attd to D/184)

A/174 + C/174 Batteries attached to "C" Group under the Command of Lui Colonel A.M Kennard DSO.
for to-day purposes.

Positions:- Group Hqrs. F.10.b.5.2.
A/184 (Captain Ramsay + Capt. Robertson) F.10.d.5.6.
D/174 (Capt. Thomas) A.13.6.5.4.
B/184 + ½ C/184 (Capt. Kamp) F.11.d.4.4.
A/186 (Major Phillips) F.5.c.5.6.
½ C/184 (att D/184)(Major Spencer) F.s.d.5.6.
½ B/186 (Capt. Tyler) X.24.c.2.5. A.D.S.S./Forms/C.2118.
B/174 (Major Nicholson) X.24.c.6.9. Enfilade Battery

"C" Group: A/174 at X.22.d.6.6. (Capt. Rouse)
C/174 at S.14.c.1.7. (Capt. Jackson)

30.4.16. [signature] Lt Colonel R.F.A.
Comdg. 174 Brigade R.F.A.

WAR DIARY
or
INTELLIGENCE SUMMARY

Sheet 14 Army Form C. 2118.

(Erase heading not required.)

Place	Date	Hour	Summary of Events and Information	Remarks and references to Appendices
GORRE	15.4.16		"B" Group covering GIVENCHY section – Subsections B1 + B2. Trench	Ref. Combined BÉTHUNE sheet 40,000
			"C" Group covering FESTUBERT section. From A16c 5½.6½ To A3.6.2.0.	Also Trench Map No.1 N.W. Ed. 6. 10,000
	16.4.16		Batteries registered in afternoon, after rounds.	
	17.4.16		Registered – 100 rounds (approx.)	
			Very little firing by own Artillery. Quiet day.	
	18.4.16		Registered – 100 rounds (approx.) Lieut E.G. Gothard RFA and 2/Lieut G.P. Shaw RFA (wounded slightly)	
			Little firing by own Artillery. Hostile shelling of GIVENCHY + FESTUBERT. 3 Bons C Batteries respectively	
	19.4.16		2/Lt C.G. VANDYK ("B" Battery) wounded with 2 Telephonists at 9·30 am - while observing	
			from BREWERY CORNER – FESTUBERT – 77 mm shrapnel – direct hit on house.	
	20.4.16		Registered – about 160 rounds.	
	21.4.16		Registration.	
		9 pm – 9·30 pm	Batteries (A/184, B/184, A/186 + B/174 & B/174) fired salvoes on front + communication	
			trenches. Retaliation by Germans during night.	
	22.4.16		Quiet day. Little shooting.	
	23.4.16		Batteries fired about 70 rounds. Registration of snipers.	
		From 1·30 pm till dark – enemy shelling west end of Tuning Fork with 5.9's – near D/184.	
	24.4.16		Registration etc. Batteries fired 140 rounds (approx.)	
	25.4.16		B/174 registering with Aeroplane. (10th Flying Squadron R.F.C.)	
		5 am –	Batteries fired on front trenches with successful result. (about 100 rds.)	
		10 pm – 11.30 pm	Division on our right had heavy bombardment by their Artillery, + Raid attempted by Infantry – with apparent good result.	30.4.16 [signature]

Army Form C. 2118.

Sheet 15.

WAR DIARY
or
INTELLIGENCE SUMMARY.
(Erase heading not required.)

Instructions regarding War Diaries and Intelligence Summaries are contained in F. S. Regs., Part II. and the Staff Manual respectively. Title pages will be prepared in manuscript.

Place	Date	Hour	Summary of Events and Information	Remarks and references to Appendices
GIVENCHY	26.4.16.		Batteries fired very little during day. Enemy shelling at 11pm GIVENCHY. 1 Direct hit into 5.9" on ARTILLERY HOUSE. Little damage. No casualties.	Ref map Combined Sheet BETHUNE 1/40000. Also Trench Map No 1 N.W. Ed. 6. 1/10,000.
	27.4.16.		From 5am - 8am. Gas attack near LOOS & HULLUCH on our right. Gas was smelt over ANNEQUIN. 4pm - 5:30pm. A/186 registered with Aeroplane on 1st Crater. A/184, B/184 & B/174 registered. Trench Mortars also fired on front & communication Trenches. Successful practice.	
	28.4.16.	8.45 pm	1st Gas alarm given by Infantry in front of GIVENCHY. All Batteries fired on front Trenches for 2.5 minutes at slow rate of fire. False alarm.	
		9.25pm	2nd Gas alarm given — Batteries fired for ¼ hr at slow rate of fire. Over 400 rds fired altogether — False alarm. Slight smell of gas was smelt in front trenches — from the south. Batteries fired little, except A/186 - who fired with Lt T Proton at new saps at A16c.67. (100 rds)	
	29.4.16.		Enemy quiet. Batteries fired little.	
	30.4.16.		Quiet day. Batteries fired little, quiet much hostile shelling.	

Bty.	Observation Post.	Zones covered.
A/184	FENTON'S FOLLY in GIVENCHY.	A9d.8.5 to A9d.5.9½.
D/174	Gunner's siding & Sappers Mess.	A16c.5.6½ to A16a.2..8.
B/184	FENTON'S FOLLY & ARTILLERY HOUSE.	A16a.3.7 to A9d.8.5.
D/184	W House - LE PLANTIN.	A9b.5.5 to A36.2.0.
B/174	BREWERY CORNER d- FESTUBERT	A9d.7.6 to A9b.5.8.
A/186	BELLEVUE in GIVENCHY	A16a.3.7 to A36.2.0.
C/B/186	No 39 in FESTUBERT.	A16c.5.4 to A9d.5.8.

30-4-16

39th Divisional Artillery.

174th BRIGADE

ROYAL FIELD ARTILLERY.

MAY 1916

Army Form C. 2118

SHEET 16

174 RFA
VOL 3

WAR DIARY or INTELLIGENCE SUMMARY

(Erase heading not required.)

Place	Date	Hour	Summary of Events and Information	Remarks and references to Appendices
GIVENCHY.	1/5/16		Quiet day - very little registration or hostile fire.	Ref. Trench Map No.1 N.W. Edition 6 1/10,000 and Combined BETHUNE Sheet, 1/40,000
	2/5/16		Lieut T.D. COLES (A/184) died in C.C.S. from concussion of the brain due to injuries sustained from a fall off his horse on the night 30/1st. Quiet day - very little firing.	
	3/5/16	7pm-7.30pm	A/186, D/174 + Light Trench Mortars fired at M.G. emplacement and support Trenches at A16c 5½ 6½ with good results. "B" group did not fire, but "C" group on our left retaliated.	
		10pm	False gas alarm. During morning D/184 registered with aeroplane.	
	4/5/16		Quiet day - very little registration or hostile fire.	
	5/5/16		Quiet day. B/174 ranged with aeroplane in morning, + D/184 with aeroplane at 1pm on A11a.	
	6/5/16 to 9/5/16		Very little hostile fire.	
	10/5/16		Ordinary routine. Little Registration or hostile fire. Quiet days.	
	11/5/16		Hostile Mine sprung at 4.30pm near Northern Craters - Some shelling of GIVENCHY Keep.	
	12/5/16	4.25am 4.35am	Mine sprung on our front - but no action. Several hostile mines sprung on our front + Communication trenches. A/186, B/184 + D/174 fired about 100 yds behind THE M Front + Communication Trenches in A10c + A10a. "b" Group, "B" Group, + 174th Bde Hdqs moved back into rest Billets	
		10 am	184th Bde Hdqrs Took over "B" Group, + 174th Bde Hdqs moved back into rest Billets at X13 a 9.4 near LOCON.	
LOCON	13/5/16 to 24.5.16		In Reserve Billets. By 20.5.16. Reorganization of Divl. Arty was complete. B.A.C. was abolished. East Bde consists of 3 18pr B.Cys and 1 4.5" How Bty. 174th Bde RFA consists of A/174, B/174 (late D/174) + D/174 (late A/186 How). B/174 becomes A/186.	G.F. Kitchell Lt Col R.F.A.
GIVENCHY	25/5/16	10.30am	174th Bde HQ took over "B" Group from 184th Bde HQ. Group consisting of 5 18pr Btys: C/184 (late A/184), B/186 (late A/186) B/184, B/174 (late D/174), B/184 (late D/174) + A/186 (late B/174). + 1 4.5" How Bty. D/174 (late A/186).	for Lt-Col RFA in Bde 174th RFA
	26/5/16	5pm 10.6pm 11.45pm	Small Operation with T.M.'s on Duck's Bill Front Trenches + Support Trenches in A9 + A10c. A/186, B/186 + D/174 fired about 120 rds (Comb) 174 RFA.	31.5.16

1875 Wt. W593/826 1,000,000 4/15 J.B.C. & A. A.D.S.S./Forms/C. 2118.

WAR DIARY
or
INTELLIGENCE SUMMARY.

Army Form C. 2118.

Sheet 17.

Place	Date	Hour	Summary of Events and Information	Remarks and references to Appendices
GIVENCHY	27.5.16		Quiet day - Little firing -	Ref Trench Map No.1. N.W. Ed. 6.
	28.5.16	6 am	Hostile Mini sprung near Duck's Bill - but no damage done - Some reputation by Battries - B/154 wire cutting N. of Duck's Bill.	1/10,000
	29.5.16	6.30 am	GIVENCHY KEEP shelled by 77 mm & 4.2" - about 70 rounds.	Combined BETHUNE sheet
	30.5.16		Quiet day on our Front - Considerable hostile shelling from trenches N. of FESTUBERT from 7 pm - 9 pm.	1/40,000
	31.5.16		Quiet day. B/174 did some Wire Cutting at A16a 3/4. 7 1/2.	

G.K.R Nash Lt Adjt
for Lt-Col RFA
Comdg 174th Bde RFA

31.5.16.

39th Divisional Artillery.

174th BRIGADE

ROYAL FIELD ARTILLERY.

JUNE 1916::

ORIGINAL

June

XXXIX WAR DIARY 174th Brigade R.F.A. Vol 4

INTELLIGENCE SUMMARY
(Erase heading not required.)

Army Form C. 2118

Instructions regarding War Diaries and Intelligence Summaries are contained in F. S. Regs., Part II. and the Staff Manual respectively. Title Pages will be prepared in manuscript.

Place	Date	Hour	Summary of Events and Information	Remarks and references to Appendices
GIVENCHY	1-6-16		Quiet day.	Ref. Trench Map Ed. 6. M.W. No. 1. 1/10,000
	2-6-16 3-6-16		B/174 & B/186 did preliminary wire cutting just south of Duck's Bill.	+ Combined BETHUNE Sheet 1 1/40,000
	4-6-16	3.30 p.m.	B/174 did some wire cutting	
		10.10 p.m. – 10.15 p.m.	Intense bombardment by Batteries of 2 B.Group :- B/174 & B/186 Wire cutting & Front Trench from A.9.d.9.2.½.6 to at Front Trench. A.10.c.½.0 :- C/186 & D/174 (How's) on Front Trench - A/186 (Enfilade) on left flank.	
		10.10 p.m.	We blew a mine in A.9.d. central.	
		10.15 p.m.	We blew a 2nd mine	
		10.15 p.m.	Raiding parts of 4 officers & 70 men of K.R.R.C. (17th Bn) went over & raided German front line trenches about A.10.c.1.½. on the flanks -	Ref. Trench Map Ed. 7. N.W. No. 1. 1/10,000
		10.17 p.m. to 11.20 p.m.	Artillery lifted & alligned formed a barrage on support trenches. 3 blocks of party on each flank. Raiders accounted for 20-25 Germans. No prisoners taken. Raiders returned to our trenches but only 5 casualties - 1 off & 4 men wounded. Fired over 1200 rds in all. (B/174 about 560 rds & B/186 about 340 rds.). Enemy retaliation only commenced at 10.30 p.m. & was very weak. Enemy front line trenches were well destroyed. Raid was very successful - Artillery cooperation excellent -	+ Combined BETHUNE Sheet 1 1/40,000
	5-6-16 6-6-16 to 16-6-16		Very quiet day. Quiet days.	
"	17-6-16	1 a.m. -1.8	Bombardment & wire cutting about A16.c.5.7 by B/174, B/186 - & cooperation by A/186, C/186 & D/174 & some Batteries of 33rd Divnl Arty. Raiders (about 40 men of Black Watch 1/s) went in at 1.8 - Raid was very successful. From 1.9 a.m. - 1.45 a.m. barrage was formed by guns - 2 Mins went up on left. Artillery fire accurate. Raiders accounted for at least 12 Germans killed - Our Casualties 6 - 1 Wounded prisoner taken of 244th Reg. Rft. Batteries fired about 1500 rounds	
	17-6-16 -19-6-16	10 a.m. -10 a.m.	Headquarters moved out of GIVENCHY GROUP (33rd Divnl Arty took over) - Reliefs & Bns & personnel of 34°.33½ - 35th Divnl Arty's took place. Took over FERME DuBois GROUP. (B/174 at S70.71.6. C/184 (Enfilade) at M34.c.5.3. A/186 at S1.d.4.8. (from 35th Divnl Arty). D/174 at M31.b.9.2.6. (3 guns) + 1 gun at F14.d.6.9.	(contd)

1875 Wt. W593/826 1,000,000 4/15 J.B.C. & A. A.D.S.S./Forms/C. 2118.

ORIGINAL

WAR DIARY 174 Bde R.F.A
or
INTELLIGENCE SUMMARY II

Army Form C. 2118

Instructions regarding War Diaries and Intelligence Summaries are contained in F.S. Regs., Part II. and the Staff Manual respectively. Title Pages will be prepared in manuscript. (cont'd)

(Erase heading not required.)

Place	Date	Hour	Summary of Events and Information	Remarks and references to Appendices
RICHEBOURG	19.6.16.	10 am	B/186 at M26.a.3.0. B/174 at N32.c.4.3. D/157 at X12.a.8.8.) Covering from S/16c 7½.2. to S11.6.2.2. Group HQ. at LACOUTURE. 116th Inf Bde. (S. 15th Bde + 2. 4·5" How. B/172 J.)	Ref. Trench 17p.Ed.7. N.W.No1. ___ 10000. & Centralized BETHUNE Sheet 1 ___ 40000.
	19.6.16 to 28.6.16		Registration by Batteries.	
	27.6.16.		B/186 moved into Wire cutting Position at S36.t.9t.	
	29.6.16.	2pm to 5pm.	Preliminary Phase – Batteries & "F" Group Wire cutting & bombardment of Front trenches about S/16a 5.7 to S10.c.9½.3. Parapet demolished wire cut. 2 Pauses from 3pm – 3.10pm & 4pm – 4.10pm. In cooperation 4 Batteries (3.15p. + 1.4.5" How) of "S" Group in support. "F" Group fired 6000 rds approx.	
	30.6.16.	2.50am to 3.5am.	Intense bombardment of front trenches + wire + parapet.	
		3.5 am.	Infantry assault. 2 Mins sporing on left of attack. (Bg 12th & 13th Bn. Royal Sussex Regt. 116 Inf Bde.)	
		3.5 am to 3.25 am	Guns lifted + formed intense close barrage on support Trenches.	
		3.25 am to 7am	Guns formed barrage on support Trenches. Infantry took 1st + 2nd lines of Trenches, but met strong German resistance & heavy O.G. fire at 3 am – after severe fighting in trenches they had to withdraw to original trenches. Hostile Artillery fire v. heavy on our front Trenches & on all O.P's especially "FACTORY" in Rue du Bois. Casualties about 1000 in all – About 4 or 6 German prisoners taken. German trenches have been reinforced by fresh troops + guns during night 29/30. Guns fired about 12000 rds between 2am 29th + 7.30 am. 30th.	
	1.7.16		V. quiet day. Collecting wounded etc. D/157 + supporting Batteries of S. Group went out at J. D/184 came into Group at X17.d.9.7.	

G.H.W. Nicholls Lt CA
RPA Bde RFA
Coul 8/7/14

39th Divisional Artillery.

174th BRIGADE

ROYAL FIELD ARTILLERY.

JULY 1916

1.

H.Q.
39th Div: Arty

Herewith Sheets 15-16 (ORIGINAL) of War Diary
for period 1st – 31st July 1916.

In the Field.
31/7/1916.

G.H.K Winch 2 Lt & adjt
for Lt Colonel R.F.A.
Commanding 174th Bde RFA

ORIGINAL

July 1916.

Army Form C. 2118.

WAR DIARY
or
INTELLIGENCE SUMMARY.
(Erase heading not required.)

Title pages July 1916. No 15

Instructions regarding War Diaries and Intelligence Summaries are contained in F. S. Regs., Part II. and the Staff Manual respectively. Title pages will be prepared in manuscript.

VIII - 5

Place	Date	Hour	Summary of Events and Information	Remarks and references to Appendices
RICHEBOURG	1.7.16 to 6.7.16		Quiet on our front. Usual Registration by Batteries - Some Hostile Shelling.	Offensive started on SOMME by 4th & 3rd Armies & French. Ref. Trench Map 1/10000 RICHEBOURG Ed. 7A.
	6.7.16.		Day & night. Relays of guns & personnel took place.	
	7.7.16.	12 noon	Handed over FERME du BOIS Group to 61st Division. Took over GIVENCHY Group from 33rd Division. 174th Bde. HQ. at Canal House. F/06's 2.	Combined BETHUNE & Sheet 40,000
		6 pm	Group consisted of 4 15th Bth. (B/174 at A136.5.4.; C/174 at F18.a.3.1.; B/156 at F16d.4.4.; C/156 at F10d.8.6 = 16 guns) + 1 4.5" How Bty. (D/179 at F5c.5.6.)	Reg. Trench Map. 1/10,000 LAPASSÉE & LAVENTIE Ed. 7A
	7.7.16. 8.7.16.	4.30 pm to 2.30 am	Shelling by 4.2" Hows. of Canal Bank near Group H.Q.. Registration	Combined "BETHUNE" Sheet as above
	9.7.16			
	10.7.16	12 noon	Group HQ. handed over to 154th Bde. HQ. & went with Battalion to 31 Rue Fantelle BETHUNE.	
	10.7.16 to 21.7.16		HQ. 174th Bde. RFA. Resting in Billets in BETHUNE.	
	15.7.16.		B/Lt. ARudge went to SAILLY to HQ. RA. of ANZAC Corps. to assist them. & Lt. Windy went to Group HQ. at LACOUTURE. (179th Bde HQ.) & Lt. Diamond	
	18.7.16 20.7.16.		Lieut. Windy left to BETHUNE. Lt. Col. ARudge left for ANZACS.	
	25/26.7.16.		B/174 came out to rest near Mt Bernenchon. (W2a). A/174, C/174 & C/174 grouped in B (Givinchy) Group). (B/174 remaining ; A/174 at F10d.7.6; C/174 at F1d.4.4).	
	27.7.16		Capt. 25th H. Rose posted to DAC. in temporary in command (A/174)	

[signed] Lt. Colonel RA Commdg. 174th Bde RFA

Army Form C. 2118

WAR DIARY
or
INTELLIGENCE SUMMARY

July 1916 No. 16.

(Erase heading not required.)

Instructions regarding War Diaries and Intelligence Summaries are contained in F.S. Regs., Part II and the Staff Manual respectively. Title Pages will be prepared in manuscript.

Place	Date	Hour	Summary of Events and Information	Remarks and references to Appendices
In the Field	27/7/16		Immediate honours rewards. (C.R.O. 409-2.) $\binom{XI^{th}}{}$	
			(P.A.R.O. No 108. Para. 368. dated 17.7.16.)	
			"Under authority delegated by the General Officer Commanding in Chief, - the Corps Commanding on the 14th inst. awarded the Military Medal to the undermentioned N.C.O.'s & men, for gallantry & devotion to duty in action :-	
			No L28566 Bombardier J. Stewart . B/174 .	
			L28593 Gunner L.C. Pragnell C/174 .	
			41291 A/Bomb. T. Fanning B/174 . "	
			No 32091 Sergt. L.J. Byrne C/174 awarded D.C. Medal 27/4/1916. (not First Army list A/1109 of 27/4/1916.)	
	28/7/16		"Lieut Jr. Sim B/174 (attached 1/39 Trench Mortar Battery) awarded The Military Cross under authority granted by His Majesty The King. (Vide 39th DRO 317 dated 28/7/16)	
	29-31/7/16		HQ 174 remaining in Rest billet at BETHUNE.	

Cavendish
Lt. Col. R.A.
Comdg. 174 Bde R.A.

39th Divisional Artillery.

174th BRIGADE.

ROYAL FIELD ARTILLERY.

AUGUST 1 9 1 6

174 Brigade RFA
August 1916

Army Form C. 2118

WAR DIARY or INTELLIGENCE SUMMARY

(Erase heading not required.)

Vol 6 Sheet 17

Instructions regarding War Diaries and Intelligence Summaries are contained in F.S. Regs., Part II. and the Staff Manual respectively. Title Pages will be prepared in manuscript.

Place	Date	Hour	Summary of Events and Information	Remarks and references to Appendices
BETHUNE	1.8.16 to 6.8.16		174 Bde HQ resting in billets in BETHUNE. B/174 roofing at MT. BERNENCHON. (W1 a 6.8.) Other batteries in action in GIVENCHY Grp.	Ref Cambrai BETHUNE Sheet 1/40000
	7.8.16		Bde HQ moved to billets at MT. BERNENCHON.	Ref. LENS Map 1/100000
MORINS	During night 9/10 & 10/11		Batteries moved out of action, & moved to billets at ECQUEDECQUES.	& HAZEBROUCK 5⋅A, Map 1/10000
	11.8.16 -12.8.16		at ECQUEDECQUES & Bde HQ	
	Night 12/13.		Bde & Brigade moved into Camp at ST. MICHEL near ST. POL.	
	13.8.16 to 20.8.16		Brigade trained in MONCHY BRETON AREA.	
	21.8.16		Brigade moved South to LUCHEUX - into billets.	
	22.8.16		Brigade moved 7 miles south into billets at FAMECHON.	
	23.8.16 to 24.8.16		At FAMECHON.	
MAILLY - ENGELBELMER	25.8.16 Nights 25/26	11am	Brigade moved into Wagon Lines at BERTRANCOURT. 18 pr. Batteries, as under, moved up into action (A Group) - between MAILLY & ENGELBELMER in front of BEAUMONT-HAMEL.	Ref. Maps 57 D France 1/40000 1/20000 Also Trench Map BEAUMONT 1/10000 & Trench Map BEAUCOURT 1/5000
ON R. ANCRE.			B/174 + ½ A/174 ⎱ Q 13d C/174 + ½ A/174 ⎰ A/179 + ½ C/179 ⎱ Q 14a B/179 + ½ C/179 ⎰ Q 14c. Group HQ at Q13d.4.8.	

Army Form C. 2118

174" Brigade R.F.A.
August 1916
Sheet 18

WAR DIARY
or
INTELLIGENCE SUMMARY
(Erase heading not required.)

Instructions regarding War Diaries and Intelligence Summaries are contained in F.S. Regs., Part II. and the Staff Manual respectively. Title Pages will be prepared in manuscript.

Place	Date	Hour	Summary of Events and Information	Remarks and references to Appendices
MAILLY	26.8.16		Registration by 18 pr Batteries on Trenches in Q.17.b.	Ref. Trench Maps etc. (see Page I)
	27.8.16	8 am	B/174 & ½ B/184 came up into action at Q.19.b. Registered. A/Bty consisted of 24 15pr guns & 6 4.5" Hows under Lt. Col. Allardyce. (R Group on our right under Lt. Col. Kilner).	
	28.8.16		Registration.	
	29.8.16	3.15 pm to 3.30 pm	Bombardment of Front Line & Support Trenches in Q.17.b.	
	30.8.16	8.30 am to 8.48 am	Ditto.	
	31.8.16 to 1.9.16	9 pm to 5 am on 1.9.16	18 pr Batteries (B/174, C/174, A/179, B/179) fired off 4 rounds gunfire on 2nd & 3rd German wires & C.T.'s in these Zones (Q.17.b.).	

[signature] 1.9.16

[signature] 1.9.16

39th Divisional Artillery.

174th BRIGADE

ROYAL FIELD ARTILLERY.

SEPTEMBER 1916

CONFIDENTIAL

WAR DIARY

of

174th Brigade, Royal Field Artillery

from 1st September 1916 to 30th September 1916

Sheets. 19 - 20.

WAR DIARY / INTELLIGENCE SUMMARY

Army Form C. 2118

174th Brigade R.F.A. 39th Div. Art.

SEPTEMBER 1916. Sheet 19.

Place	Date	Hour	Summary of Events and Information	Remarks and references to Appendices
MAILLY	1.9.16	9.0 pm	18 pdr Batteries (B/174 C/174 A/149 B/149) Burst of fire on 2nd Ger Line wire O C 7 S	Ref Trench Map BEAUMONT HAMEL 1:10,000 "BEAUCOURT" 1:5000
	2.9.16	5.30 am – 6.30 am	Xmas Zone (Pry G)	
			Bombardment of Zone Support Trenches in Q/176.	
	3.9.16	6.15 am	Bombardment of Enemy Support Trenches in Q/176 by groups of Heavy Ty 25 yards at a time to cmnct. Infantry assault.	
		6.19 am	Formed Barrage round point of entry	
		=12 noon		
	4.9.16		— No action.	
	5.9.16	all day	Wire Cutting Q 11 c 33 - H.S.	
	6.9.16	"	In action.	
	7.9.16	"	" "	
	8.9.16	"	" "	
	9.9.16	"	" "	
	10.9.16	"	" "	
	11.9.16	"	" "	
	12.9.16	"	" "	
	13.9.16	"	" "	
	14.9.16	"	" "	
	15.9.16	"	" "	
	16.9.16	"	Routine firing	
	17.9.16	"	In action	

1/4 Bde RJA. 39th Div Arty.

September 1916 Sheet 20

WAR DIARY
or
INTELLIGENCE SUMMARY
(Erase heading not required.)

Army Form C. 2118

Instructions regarding War Diaries and Intelligence Summaries are contained in F. S. Regs., Part II. and the Staff Manual respectively. Title Pages will be prepared in manuscript.

Place	Date	Hour	Summary of Events and Information	Remarks and references to Appendices
MAILLY	19.9.16		In action.	
"	20.9.16		Group Headquarters moved to Engebelmer Shopnah. Command of Pt. Group. 39th Divn.	A/174, B/174, C/174, D/174. R/184 A/186, B/186, D/186 ?
	21.9.16		Registering New Zones	
	22.9.16		In action	
	23.9.16		In action	
	24.9.16		In action	
	25.9.16		In action	
	26.9.16		In action	
	27.9.16		In action	
	28.9.16		In action in support of attack by Canadian Corps & 2nd Corps	
	29.9.16		Headquarters moved to Q25-a 9.3. Many days firing	
	29.9.16		In action	
	30.9.16		Co-operated in attack by 18th & 49th Divns.	

James Ellis
Lt. Col.
1/4 RJA

39th Divisional Artillery.

174th BRIGADE

ROYAL FIELD ARTILLERY.

OCTOBER 1 9 1 6

WAR DIARY or INTELLIGENCE SUMMARY

Army Form C. 2118

17th Brigade R.F.A.

Vol. 1. Sheet No. 21. October 1st – 31st 1916. 39th Div.

Place	Date	Hour	Summary of Events and Information	Remarks and references to Appendices
P25d 9.3	1.10.16	—	In action. Batteries engaged in enemy & keeping under fire approaches to SERRE & BEAUMONT HAMEL & THIEPVAL in P24d & R19a.	Ref Map 57dSE BEAUMONT 1/10000
	2.10.16	"	In action	
	3.10.16	"	"	
	4.10.16	"	"	
	5.10.16	"	"	
	6.10.16	"	"	
	7.10.16	"	"	
	8.10.16	"	"	
	9.10.16	"	"	
	10.10.16	"	"	
	11.10.16	"	"	
	12.10.16	"	"	
	13.10.16	"	"	
	14.10.16	"	"	
	15.10.16	"	"	
	16.7.16	"	"	Relieved
	17.10.16	"	Continued in support of Infantry. Arrived at Schwaben Redoubt by R31d.	
	18.10.16	3.0pm	Brigade moved to P25d 9.3 arrived at 10pm	
		4.0pm	Relieved by 118th Inf Bdy 39 Div. at 10.30pm orders were received	
	19.10.16	9.30 am	Returned to P25d 9.3.	
	20.10.16	"	In action. Wire cutting in P4G & P15.C. all day	
	21.10.16	"	"	
	22.10.16	"	Attacked K63 to Tactical Control. Guns cutting again all day	
	23.10.16		Registered Battle Zone & Entry & Exit Wire cut on it.	
	24.10.16		In action. During 10 hrs day of C4/144 bagged 95 Huns emerging from Java 27. Sf 452	
	25.10.16			
	26.10.16			C17a P8a P2 in P24d
– 31.10.16				

12th Bde.
4th Division.

WAR DIARY

2nd LANCASHIRE FUSILIERS

....

1 9 1 5

39th Divisional Artillery.

174th BRIGADE

ROYAL FIELD ARTILLERY.

NOVEMBER 1 9 1 6

174 Brigade R.F.A.

War Diary — Sheet 22-23.

for Period. 1/11/16 — 30/11/16.

Army Form C. 2118.

WAR DIARY
or
INTELLIGENCE SUMMARY.

174th Brigade R.F.A. Diary No. 22. Nov. 1st 1916 to 18.11.16

(Erase heading not required.)

Instructions regarding War Diaries and Intelligence Summaries are contained in F. S. Regs., Part II. and the Staff Manual respectively. Title pages will be prepared in manuscript.

Place	Date	Hour	Summary of Events and Information	Remarks and references to Appendices
Q.25d.9.3	1/11/16		In Action	Ref 3rd SE
	2/11/16		do	
	3/11/16		do	
	4/11/16		do	
	5/11/16		do	
	6/11/16		do	
	7/11/16		do	
	8/11/16		do	
	9/11/16		do	
	10/11/16		do	
	11/11/16		do	
	12/11/16		do	
	13/11/16	6.15 AM	Co-operated in support of 63rd R.N.D. in attack on German trenches immediately N of R. Ancre. Heavy days firing all day. Battle continued. B/174 moved to advanced position in A6c. Battery heavily shelled with gas shells during advance	
	14/11/16		Entrance of Ancre in support of Infantry.	
	15/11/16		Both Heros advanced to "HAMEL". 3/4 Boe A/174 forced under command	
	16/11/16		of 174 Bde. Firing all day.	
	17/11/16		In action.	
	18/11/16	3.0 pm	Attack in Support of Attack on Muck TRENCH.	

WAR DIARY or INTELLIGENCE SUMMARY

Army Form C. 2118.

174 Brigade R.F.A.

Sheet No 23. Nov. 19/11/16 – 30.11.16

Place	Date	Hour	Summary of Events and Information	Remarks and references to Appendices
HAMEL	19.11.16	3.0 p	Cooperated in attack on strong point at junction of MUCK & LEWE TRENCHES.	Ref 54 SFG. 10,000
		5 pm	Withdrew out of action to HEADAUVILLE.	Ref LENS. 1:40,000
	20.11.16	10 AM	Bde Marched to AMPLIER	
	21.11.16	"	" AGROMETZ	
	22.11.16	"	" MONCHY CAYEUX	
	23.11.16	"	Resting at MONCHY CAYEUX	
	24.11.16	"		
	25.11.16	9.15 AM	" LIGNY LEZ AIRE	
	26.11.16	9.30 AM	" BIEENBECQUE	Ref AZEBROUCK. 1:100,000
	27.11.16	"	" ARNEKE	
	28.11.16	"	Billeted at ARNEKE	
	29.11.16	"	" " "	
	30.11.16	"	" " "	

J Weudy Moe
OC 174 Br RFA.

39th Divisional Artillery.

174th BRIGADE

ROYAL FIELD ARTILLERY.

DECEMBER 1 9 1 6

War Diary

174th Brigade R.F.A.

Sheet 24   1/12/16 to 31/12/16.

1/4 Duyanne...

WAR DIARY
or
INTELLIGENCE SUMMARY

(Erase heading not required.)

Sheet 24.

Army Form C. 2118

Dec: 1st 1916 to Dec

Instructions regarding War Diaries and Intelligence Summaries are contained in F. S. Regs., Part II. and the Staff Manual respectively. Title Pages will be prepared in manuscript.

Place	Date	Hour	Summary of Events and Information	Remarks and references to Appendices
ARNEKE	1/12.16		In Rest Billets. REORGANISATION of Bde commenced.	Hazebrouck to Arneke
	2.12.16		do	
	3.12.16		do	
	4.12.16		do	
	5.12.16		do	
	6.12.16		do	
	7.12.16		do	continued.
	8.12.16		do	
	9.12.16		do	
	10.12.16		do	
	11.12.16		do	
	12.12.16		do	
	13.12.16		do	
	14.12.16	9.a.m.	ADVANCE PARTY to 38th Div. Arty.	
YPRES.	15.12.16	5pm	RELIEF of 38th Div Arty Commenced.	
SALIENT.	16.12.16	5pm	RELIEF COMPLETED.	
(LEFT).	17.12.16		HOLDING LINE — IN ACTION — Right Group 39 Div A, B, C. D/174 A/271. D/179.	
	18.12.16		do	
	19.12.16		do	
	20.12.16		do	
	21.12.16		do	
	22.12.16		do	
	23.12.16		do	
	24.12.16		do	
	25.12.16		do	
	26.12.16		do	
	27.12.16		do	
	28.12.16		do	
	29.12.16		do	
	30.12.16		do	
	31.12.16		do.	

J. Alexander Hughes
=D/174 Div. RFA.

War Diary.

174th Brigade, Royal Field Artillery.

Sheet 24.

Jan 1st 1917 to Jan 31st 1917.

174th Brigade R.G.A.

WAR DIARY or INTELLIGENCE SUMMARY

Army Form C. 2118.

SHEET 25. JAN 1 - 1917 to JAN 31 - 1917

Place	Date	Hour	Summary of Events and Information	Remarks and references to Appendices
YPES SALIENT LEFT	1.1.17		Right Group 39" S.A. A,B,C,D/174 A/174 & D/174 Holding the Line.	Recd 28 rr w +a 1/ 24 ova
	2.1.17		do	
	3.1.17		do	
	4.1.17		do	
Nr REGEESBERG	5.1.17		do	
	6.1.17		do	
	7.1.17		do	
	8.1.17		do	
	9.1.17		do	
	10.1.17		do	
	11.1.17		do	
	12.1.17		do	
	13.1.17		do	
	14.1.17		do	
	15.1.17		do	
	16.1.17		Commenced relief of 55" S.A.	
I.B.C. 1.9.	17.1.17		Relief continued	
	18.1.17		Relieved Hqrs Rt Group 55" S.A. Relief completed 7 p.m. Group Headquarters at I.B.d 1.9. A,B,C,D/174 A/2-174 C/174	
	19.1.17		do	
	20.1.17		do	
	21.1.17		do	
	22.1.17		do	
	23.1.17		do	
	24.1.17		do	
	25.1.17		do	
	26.1.17		Group Reinforced by B/245 & 4 Guns of C/244	
	27.1.17		do	
	28.1.17		do	
	29.1.17		do	
	30.1.17		do Bombarded enemy Trenches in neighbourhood of RAILWAY WOOD	
	31.1.17		do	

J Bennett Lt Col Comdg 174th Bde RGA

WAR DIARY or INTELLIGENCE SUMMARY

14th Bde R.H.A.

Army Form C. 2118.

Ref Map 28 N.W. BELGIUM SHEET 26. 1/20,000

Vol 12

Place	Date	Hour	Summary of Events and Information	Remarks and references to Appendices
YPRES	1.2.17		In action	I8d 1.9
	2.2.17		do	
	3.2.17		do	
	4.2.17		do	
	5.2.17		do	
	6.2.17		do	
	7.2.17		do	
	8.2.17		do	
	9.2.17		do	
	10.2.17		do	
	11.2.17		do	
	12.2.17		do	
	13.2.17		do	Wire cutting on mound. 15 to 6.5". commenced by A 173/74 1 H.E. each
	14.2.17	12:30 AM	Fired in support of Raid by 117 INF Bde. on the Mound	do continued
	15.2.17		In action	do arranged bombardment of Hostile Trenches during the day
	16.2.17		do	do
	17.2.17		do	do
	18.2.17		do	
	19.2.17		do	
	20.2.17		Hrs out of Action (relieved by 55 D.A.) Proceeded to Rest at WATOU.	
	21.2.17		In Rest at WATOU. A,B,C, H.Q at WATOU - D/74 at HOUTKERQUE	Sheet 27. 1/40,000
	22.2.17		do	
	23.2.17		do	
	24.2.17		do	
	25.2.17		do	
	26.2.17		do	
	27.2.17		do	
	28.2.17		do	

A Trenfett Lt
for Lt Col Cmdg
14th Bde R.H.A.

174" Brigade, R.F.A.

Army Form C. 2118.

WAR DIARY
or
INTELLIGENCE SUMMARY.
(Erase heading not required.)

Ref. map 28 N.W. Sheet 27. 1/20,000 Belgium

Place	Date	Hour	Summary of Events and Information	Remarks and references to Appendices
YPRES.	1.3.17		In action	Relieved 23rd Div. A.Cy. – (Observatory Ridge Section) Vol I. 114 q.2.
	2.3.17		do	
	3.3.17		do	
	4.3.17		do	
	5.3.17		do	
	6.3.17		do	
	7.3.17		do	
	8.3.17		do	
	9.3.17		do	
	10.3.17		do	
	11.3.17		do	
	12.3.17		do	
	13.3.17		do	
	14.3.17		do	
	15.3.17		do	
	16.3.17		do	
	17.3.17		do	
	18.3.17		do	
	19.3.17		do	
	20.3.17		do	12.30 a.m. Enemy attempted raid on I.30.b. Driven off. A.61/7 lus.
	21.3.17		do	
	22.3.17		do	
	23.3.17		do	
	24.3.17		do	B1/4 (I.7.b.20.) shell heavy – One gun off/u put out of action. 2 men wounded.
	25.3.17		do	
	26.3.17		do	
	27.3.17		do	
	28.3.17		do	
	29.3.17		do	
	30.3.17		do	
	31.3.17		do	No damage.

HQ 174 Bde RFA.

WAR DIARY
or
INTELLIGENCE SUMMARY
(Erase heading not required.)

Army Form C. 2118

Sheet No. 28.
1/4/17 to 30/4/17

Jul 14

Instructions regarding War Diaries and Intelligence Summaries are contained in F. S. Regs., Part II. and the Staff Manual respectively. Title Pages will be prepared in manuscript.

Place	Date	Hour	Summary of Events and Information	Remarks and references to Appendices
LILLE GATE YPRES	1·4·17		In action	2. Ypres 4A 1 – 10,000
	2·4·17		do	
	3·4·17		do	
	4·4·17		do	
	5·4·17		do	
	6·4·17		do	
	7·4·17		do	
	8·4·17		Cooperated with 49th Divn in raid on Hill 60 sector.	
	9·4·17		Section withdrew from action to VIII Corps Reserve area.	
HOUTKERQUE	10·4·17		Remaining sections withdrew during the night, the enemy attempted shell our trenches. Batteries were called on for support.	Ref Hazebrouck 5A 1 – 100,000
	11·4·17		Bde HQ 2 A/174 at Houtkerque.	
	12·4·17		B, C, D/174 at Watou.	
	13·4·17		Training commenced	
	14·4·17		do continued	
	15·4·17		do	
	16·4·17		do	
	17·4·17		do	
LEDERZEELE LICQUES WISSANT	18·4·17		Marched under orders from II Army to Leserzeele en route for Wissant area.	
	19·4·17		Marched continued to Licques.	
	20·4·17		do Wissant	Calais 13 1/100,000
	21·4·17		Training commenced	
	22·4·17		do continued	
	23·4·17		do	
	24·4·17		do	
	25·4·17		do	
	26·4·17		do	
	27·4·17		do	
	28·4·17		do	
	30·4·17		do	

174th Army R.E.

WAR DIARY
or
INTELLIGENCE SUMMARY.
(Erase heading not required.)

Army Form C. 2118.

Sheet No. 29. 1/5/1917 – 31/5/1917.

Hour, Date, Place	Summary of Events and Information	Remarks and references to Appendices
May 1st 1917 WISSANT 1.30 AM	Regt. Training Regt. Marquise – RINXENT	Map CALAIS Sheets 13
2nd "	Bde marched to LICQUES	do
3rd " LICQUES	do do LEMPIRE 10th Bn. RECOUPE – ST MOMELIN	to HAZEBROUCK 54.
4th " KEMMERELIS	do do WATOU Bn. WINNEZEELE Chapel	do
5th " WATOU	do do in the line	ST JULIEN 20 NW. ed 54.
6th " do	2 Secs A, B, C, D relieved Composites 20ct 122 Bde in the line	do
7th "	Remaining secs + HQ relieved 122 HQ at RIEGERSBURG Map as	do
8th	Etres "R" Group A B C D 174 Bde A/298 C/298 AFWO D/76	do
9th	In action	attached 55 Div. do
10	do	do
11	do	do
12	do	do
13	do	do
14	do	do
15	do	do
16	Cooperated with 118th Inf Bde in raid on CANADIAN Tr. 2 Prisoners	do
17	In action	(Bavarians) do
18	do	do
19	do	do
20	do	do
21	2 secs B/86 + C/186 relieved 2 Secs. A/298 + C/298 cooperated	do
22	remaining secs relieved as above	do
23	"R" Group A B C D 174 Bde B + C/186 + B/246.	do
24	In action	do
25	do	do
26	do	do
27	HQ 186 took over from HQ 174 HQ 174 proceeded to Esquelbecq	do
28	HQ at A19 c 2.8.	do
29		
30		

WAR DIARY *or* **INTELLIGENCE SUMMARY** 1st – 30th June 1917.

Army Form C. 2118

174th Brigade R.F.A.

Ref. Sheet 28 & 29 Belgium 1/40,000

Vol 16

Place	Date	Hour	Summary of Events and Information	Remarks and references to Appendices
PESELHOEK	1.6.17		Brigade Headquarters in Reserve	
	2.6.17		Batteries in action under "R. Group" 39th Div.	
	3.6.17		do	
	4.6.17		do	
	5.6.17		do	
	6.6.17		do	
	7.6.17		do	
	8.6.17		do	
	9.6.17		do	
	10.6.17		do	
	11.6.17		do	
	12.6.17		do	
	13.6.17		do	
	14.6.17		do	
	15.6.17		do	
	16.6.17		do	
	17.6.17		do	
	18.6.17		do	
	19.6.17		do	
	20.6.17		do	
	21.6.17		do	
	22.6.17		do	
	23.6.17		do	
	24.6.17		B/174 & D/174 withdrawn from action to B.T. A.19.b.2.8. & F.24.a.9. & respectively Sheet 28	
	25.6.17		C/186 at B.30.a.4.1. being relieved by A/17 at B.29.c.4.4.	
	26.6.17		C/174 relieved C/186 at B.30.a.4.1. & heat as above	
	27.6.17		do	
	28.6.17		do	
	29.6.17		do	
	30.6.17		do	

174th Brigade, R.F.A. Sheet No. 42 Army Form C. 2118

WAR DIARY

INTELLIGENCE SUMMARY

(Erase heading not required.)

1st to 31st January, 1918.

Place	Date	Hour	Summary of Events and Information	Remarks and references to Appendices
January	1 to 3		Resting and training in NOORDPEENE Area. Hdqrs. at H29 d 3.3 A/174 " H21 c 9.5 B/174 " H30 d 8.0 C/174 " H36 d 2.5 D/174 " H32 d 0.4	Belgium & France Sheet 27, Ed. 2 1/40,000
	4		Brigade marched to the POPERINGHE Area. The move was anything but enjoyable. The hard frost of the previous week had made the roads very slippery, and - for the first hour or so after leaving NOORDPEENE - it was a common sight to see vehicles side-slipping off the road into the nearest ditch - dragging the teams with them. A/174 did not get beyond STEENVOORDE where they billeted for the night. The rest of the Brigade completed the march, and occupied camps as follows - Hdqrs. at TEN ELMS CAMP (A25 d 2.6) B/174 " A21 c 8.8 C/174 " } A20 d 3.1 D/174 " }	Belgium & France Sheet 28, Ed. 3 1/40,000

174th Brigade, R.F.A

Sheet No. 43

WAR DIARY
or
INTELLIGENCE SUMMARY

1st to 31st January, 1918

Army Form C. 2118

Place	Date	Hour	Summary of Events and Information	Remarks and references to Appendices
January	5		A/174 completed their march and occupied camp at A27d 7.0	Belgium & France Sheet 28, S.d 3 1/40.000
	6		In reserve in POPERINGHE Area.	
	7 & 8		Relieved the 168 Brigade in action.	
			H.Qrs. 174 relieved H.Qrs. 168 at C17c 42.35 (on Jan. 8)	
			A/174 relieved A/168 at D2c 78.82 (forward "sniping" gun) & D7a 45.35 (5 guns)	
			B/174 relieved B/168 at C12b 43.64	
			C/174 " C/168 " A7c 50.32 (4 guns) & D7c 10.62 (2 ")	
			D/174 relieved D/168 at C12d 68.40 (2 how.s) & C12d 90.60 (2 ")	
			Covering the Left Battalion, Right Division, II Corps (WEST ROOSEBEKE sector).	
			Wagon lines moved to BRIELEN area –	
	8		A/174 ⎫	
			B/174 ⎬ at B29d central	
			C/174 ⎭	
			H.Qrs.	
			D/174 at B22d 4.4.	

174th Brigade, R.F.A.

Sheet No. 44   Army Form C. 2118

WAR DIARY
or
INTELLIGENCE SUMMARY

(Erase heading not required.)

1st to 31st January, 1918.

Place	Date	Hour	Summary of Events and Information	Remarks and references to Appendices
January	9 to 21		In action as above.	
		11	Intense area shoot in the neighbourhood of our batteries, lasting from 12 noon to 3.30 p.m. Estimated at about 5,000 rounds, from all calibres up to 21cm. Mortar. Surprisingly few casualties (one Officer and one gunner of A/174 wounded). No guns damaged.	
	22		One section of A/174 and one section of C/174 withdrew from action.	
	23		B/174 and D/174 (one section each) relieved by 108 Battery and D/23 (23 Army Brigade) respectively. Hdqrs. 174 relieved by Hdqrs. 23 Wagon Lines moved to POPERINGHE Area – Hdqrs. at TEN ELMS CAMP (A25d 2.6) Belgium & France, Sheet 28, Ed.3, 1/40,000 A/174 " F18c 0.0 B/174 " F18a 9.1 } Belgium & France, Sheet 27, Ed.2, 1/40,000 C/174 " F18a 2.4 D/174 " F24c 9.5 Remaining guns of A/174 and C/174 withdrew from action, except "enemy" gun of A/174 – which was relieved by 108 Battery (23 Army Brigade).	
	24		Relief of B/174 and D/174 completed.	

Army Form C. 2118

WAR DIARY or INTELLIGENCE SUMMARY

(Erase heading not required)

174th Brigade, R.F.A

Sheet No. 45

1st to 31st January, 1918.

Place	Date	Hour	Summary of Events and Information	Remarks and references to Appendices
January	25 to 26		In POPERINGHE Area. Preparing for move by train to 5th Army Area. Brigade entrained at PROVEN (F.1.c.6.0) Belgium, France Sheet 27. Ed 2. 1/40.000	Trace Sheet AMIENS 17. Ed 2. 1/100.000
	27 to 28		Brigade detrained at MERICOURT-L'ABBE (I.G.8.5) and marched to billets at ETINEHEM (I.3.1.) Train journey occupied about 12 hours, and was completed without incident. Arrangements were very good and everything worked smoothly.	
	29 to 31		Re-organising at ETINEHEM.	

4-2-1918

C.S. Carr
Capt. R.F.A.
Adjt. 174 Brigade R.F.A.

174th Brigade, R.F.A.

Army Form C. 2118.

WAR DIARY
or
INTELLIGENCE SUMMARY.

Sheet No. 46

1st to 28th February, 1918.

Place	Date	Hour	Summary of Events and Information	Remarks and references to Appendices
Feb.	1		Re-organising at ETINEHEM.	
	2		Brigade moved to HAUT ALLAINES. Hqrs. at C5b0.5. Batteries at C10b.3.8.	Sheet 62c
	3		174 Brigade began the relief of 51 Brigade (9th Divisional Artillery). Completed relief of personnel of one section per Battery.	
			A/174 relieved C/51 at W17a 55.50	
			B/174 " B/51 " W9d 80.20	Sheet 57c
			C/174 " A/51 " W10a 90.05	
			D/174 " D/51 " W10a 00.80	
	4		Completed relief of personnel of remaining sections per Battery. Hqrs. 174 relieved Hqrs. 51 at W9d 65.06. Sheet 57c Hqrs. 174 assumed command of Centre Artillery Brigade, covering Centre Infantry Brigade, Left Division, VII Corps. (GOUZEAUCOURT Sector.) C/174 also man Anti-Tank gun at W6c 10.75. Sheet 57c Wagon Lines moved to W13 B 8.8. Sheet 57c	
	5, 6, 16		In action as above.	

174th Brigade, R.F.A.　　Army Form C. 2118.

WAR DIARY
INTELLIGENCE SUMMARY.

Sheet No. 47.

1st to 28th February, 1918.

Place	Date	Hour	Summary of Events and Information	Remarks and references to Appendices
Feb.	17		186 Brigade began to relieve 174th Brigade. Relief of personnel of one Section per Battery completed. A, B, C, D/174 relieved by A, B, C, D/186 respectively.	
	18		Relief of personnel of remaining two Sections per Battery completed. Hdqrs. 174 relieved by Hdqrs. 186. 174 Brigade moved to NURLU — Hdqrs. at D4a 6.9　　Sheet 62ᶜ A/174 at D28c 5.2 B/174 at } Sheet 57ᶜ C/174 at D27 central D/174	
	19 to 27		Training at NURLU.	
	28		174 Brigade proceeded into action — Hdqrs. at Q15c 70.20 A/174 at Q22c 55.75 B/174 at Q22c 52.98　} Sheet 57ᶜ C/174 at Q22a 50.80 D/174 at Q22c 29.39 Hdqrs. 174 Command Command of Left Artillery Group (65 Army Bde. and 174 Bde.), covering Left Brigade, Left Division, VII Corps. (GOUZEAUCOURT Left Section of GOUZEAU COURT Sector.)	

4.3.1918

A.S. Cave.
Capt. R.F.A.
Adjt. 174 Brigade R.F.A.

39th Div.

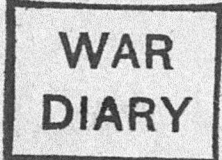

Headquarters,

174th BRIGADE, R.F.A.

M A R C H

1 9 1 8

17th BRIGADE R.F.A.

Vol 25. 1-31st March 1918

Map references from Sheet 62c 1/40000

Date	Hour		
1st March		Covering GOUZEAUCOURT LEFT Section. 17th Bde commanding Left Artillery Group (17th Bde & 65th Bde).	
3rd March 5th March 7th March 10th March		Hqrs moved to Q.34.a.5.5. Bde harassing the enemy day and night, out lying medium established Bombarded T.M. emplacements in conjunction with 9.45" T.M.s	
11th March night 11/12th night 14/15th 12th March 15th March	3 a.m.	145th Black Watch undertook the fighting patrols + Left group counterpreparation. Enemy heavies found unoccupied emplacements by concealing batteries of 50th Bde in action per battery relieved by corresponding batteries of 50th Bde. Wagon lines moved to HALLE (I.19 & J.5 - Sheet 62c). Permanent positions per battery, relieved by 50th Bde. HQ 17th Bde returned to H.19. 50th Bde - Bde in GHQ reserve.	
	4.30 pm	Bde moved to HAUT ALLAINES I.I.a. - Sheet 62c.- Batteries training and calibration at range.	
21st March	4.30 am	Intense bombardment opened on whole front. Bde ordered to stand to.	
	10.00 am	Enemy attacks on 50 mile front. Batteries in action in valley.	
	2.0 pm	Bde ordered to rendezvous 16" RAVINE. N.A. ROISEL (K.10 & 16) HQrs K.11 a.7.6 - Batteries. Enemy continues attack. Fog K.11 a T.6 - Batteries left by thick approximate - Batteries orders to withdraw. 'D' battery alone bring rifle to get guns away in time - Bde now consisted of D.17/4 (4 how) B.174 (2 guns from I.C.M.) 3 Hows of D189 and 1 gun & C/189 (attached) - 'D' battery came into action at TINCOURT (S.18.c.4..3) and did great execution among advancing enemy and material - Bde in action covering "green" (6148) line from Sig. Hqrs BOSSU -	
22nd			
23rd	8.0 am	Batteries withdrawn to T.20.c.9.9. Hqrs HALLE	
	2.30 pm	Batteries withdrawn to H.28.d & H.34.b Hqrs H.27.a. Batteries withdrew at night to H.27.c & H.33.a - Hqrs G.26.c.3.1. HAUT ALLAINES - CLEVY district. Batteries enjoying marked enemy in HAUT ALLAINES - G.31 central.	
24th			
25th		with great effect - Hqrs G.32 & 4.9 G.31 central. Enemy masses & bombardment engaged all day - Enemy crosses SOMME at HALLE & FAUBOURG de PARIS	

174 Brigade R.F.A.   1-31st March 1918.

Date	Hour		Remarks
25th	9.30pm	Batteries withdrawn to M4 c, Nq a thence DOMMIERE HOPE in M9 d – Batteries to 188 Brigade relieved – 174 Bde under Lt.-Col. WARREN 171 Bde from 9.0am to 4.0pm–	Reference Sheet 62D 1/40,000
26th	9.30am	Batteries withdrawn to Q 35 HQrs MARCOURT J.Q.34 B. A/282 attached to Bde. Enemy engaged and brought just down beyond FRAMERVILLE.	
27th	11.0am to 6pm	Batteries withdrawn to Q.33a & 32b to W1 B/D Battery in Q 32 a a	
28th		At night B/174 & A/282 took up position of readiness at Vil le enemy having entered LAMOTTE where B Section MG B/174 fire B/174 & A/282 intend to advance to position in Q.33a Grid on their way up received orders to cover the line of the railway in V.12, W.7 and therefore took up positions in V.22 & V.21. HQrs in V.07 & V.26 5-6. 7/174 & C/174 came into action with HQrs each & B/174 became a third from the Bde withdrew to positions in O.24.c & U.30a at night	
29th	2.30pm	Bde orders to cover zone from AMIENS - LAMOTTE Road & SOMME. Positions taken up in O.24 a a G and O.30 a – HQrs O.29 a.2.5 and O.27 d.6.8. Enemy movement & pre-arranged concentrations fired. Under orders of 16th D.A. through 39th D.A. Covering CAREY's force	
30th 31st		A/282 attached to 50th D.A. 16th D.A. shoots covering 1st Cav. Div. Harassing fire and hurricane bursts on concentrations carried out.	

J.R.S. Morley RFA
Adj 174 Bde

1/4/18.

39th Divisional Artillery.

174th BRIGADE R. F. A.

APRIL 1918.

174th Brigade, R.F.A. WAR DIARY

INTELLIGENCE SUMMARY. — 1st to 30th April, 1918. (4 sheets)

Army Form C. 2118.

Remarks and references to Appendices:
France
Sheet 62ᴰ Ed. 1
1/40,000

Place	Date	Hour	Summary of Events and Information
April	1 to	3	Harrassing fire by night. Concentrations by day. Much movement engaged.
		4	Enemy attacked North of AMIENS Road and captured BOIS DE VAIRE. Attack was preceded by a heavy bombardment, our line personnel and forward gun lines suffered somewhat severely. Communication between F.O.O. and Batteries was maintained, despite great difficulties. Batteries did great execution — firing all day with observed fire on masses of the enemy. A forward section in the road in P.20 a was finally rendered by the enemy, but the guns were recovery the same night. During the afternoon, further attacks developed, but were broken up by artillery fire on each occasion. After dusk, Batteries were withdrawn to positions in O.22 c, with HHqrs at MAISON du BOIS L'ABBE (O.26 d 3.0). Casualties during the day — 2 Officers wounded 3 Other ranks killed 26 " " wounded (3 of whom subsequently died) 1 " " missing
		5	No further attacks. Batteries moved to positions in vicinity of GENTELLES. HHqrs in GENTELLES (T.12 d 5.6).

Army Form C. 2118.

174th Brigade R.F.A. WAR DIARY
INTELLIGENCE SUMMARY. 1st to 30th April, 1918.

France
Sheet 62ᴰ Ed. 1
1/40.000

Place	Date	Hour	Summary of Events and Information	Remarks and references to Appendices
April	6		Batteries moved during the morning to positions in U2c and U8a. Arrival of 2nd wagons from 39th D.A.C. carrying ammunition. Considerable enemy shell in the neighbourhood of batteries. Casualties:- 1 Officer killed 1 Other rank killed 12 " " wounded	
	7		5th Australian Infantry Brigade attacked at dawn to gain the line U29 b 5.7 - U12 c 0.0 - U6 c 5.7. We supported the attack. Attack was successful but a strong counter-attack late in the day forced them back to their original line. Steady fire on movement was carried out throughout the day. Harassing fire at night.	
	8		Concentrations and steady fire by day. Harassing fire at night.	
	9		Battery positions heavily shelled all day by guns and how.s of all calibres. Similar attention given to GENTELLES. H.Q.s moved to T 6 b. Trench were attacked at dusk in neighbourhood of HANGARD. Attack was repulsed. Co-operated. After dusk, Batteries moved positions as follows:- A/174 to U16 6.1 B/174 to U1 c 7.7 D/174 to U1 c 8.2	

174th Brigade RFA

Army Form C. 2118.

WAR DIARY
or
INTELLIGENCE SUMMARY.

1st to 30th April, 1918.

(Erase heading not required.)

Place	Date	Hour	Summary of Events and Information	Remarks and references to Appendices
April	10		Harassing fire carried out continuously. Batteries moved positions as follows during the night — A/174 to U.14.d.1.6 B/174 to U.2.c.75.40 D/174 to U.14.d.00.25 3rd Battery R.F.A. (8th Divisional Artillery) moved to U.21.c.8.8 and came under our orders.	France Sheet 62ᴰ Ed.1 1/40.000
	11		Harassing fire by night. Observed fire on movement by day.	
	12		Enemy captured HANGARD from the French during the morning. Hostile attacks at dusk were completely overcome. We co-operated on each occasion. 174 Bde relieved after dusk by 307 Bde. (61st Divisional Artillery) and withdrawn to wagon lines in vicinity of BOVES. Hqrs. in BOVES (T.7) in neighbourhood of CAGNY (M.33 and 27).	
	13		A/174 and B/174 moved to AMIENS (M.21.a).	
	14		Hqrs. moved to AMIENS (M.21.a).	
	15		Brigade marched to MOLLIENS-au-BOIS (AMIENS Sheet, 1 E 65.89)	
	16		" " " SAULTY (LENS Sheet, 4 G 40.60).	
	17		" " " FOSSEUX (" " 3 G 80.10)	
18 to 28			Re-organising and re-equipping at FOSSEUX. Brigade in VI Corps Reserve.	

174th Brigade, RFA

Army Form C. 2118.

WAR DIARY
of
INTELLIGENCE SUMMARY. 1st to 30th April, 1918.
(Erase heading not required.)

Instructions regarding War Diaries and Intelligence Summaries are contained in F. S. Regs., Part II. and the Staff Manual respectively. Title pages will be prepared in manuscript.

Place	Date	Hour	Summary of Events and Information	Remarks and references to Appendices
April	29		174 Bde. relieved 155 Army Bde. as follows:— A/174 relieves A/155 at X 16 a 6.9 B/174 " B/155 " X 11 d 77.76 C/174 " C/155 " X 23 a 44.75 D/174 " D/155 " X 15 b 97.77 Relief of first two sections per Battery completed after dusk. Wagon lines moved to neighbourhood of BELLACOURT (R 31). 155 Army Bde. wagon lines taken over.	France Sheet 51C Ed. 2 1/40,000
	30		Hqrs./155 at X 13 b 1.1. Relief of remaining sections per Battery completed after dusk. Hqrs./174 relieves Hqrs. of 155 Army Bde. RFA. 174 controls Right group of 40th Divisional Artillery. Right group consists of 4 batteries of 174 Bde. RFA. "T" Battery R.H.A. and C/181 (40th D.A.). Covering 99th Infantry Brigade (2nd Division), which is the Right Brigade of 2nd Division front. Zone — S 27 a 0.2 to road in S 28 n (Sheet 51 B).	O.C. 40th RFA Adjt. 174 Bde. RFA 1/5/18

34

174th Bde R.F.A.

Army Form C. 2118.

WAR DIARY 1st to 31st May 1918
or
INTELLIGENCE SUMMARY.
(Erase heading not required.)

Vol 257

Remarks and references to Appendices

Reference Sheets 51a SE and 51 B SW.
1 : 20,000.

Place	Date	Hour	Summary of Events and Information
	1.5.18		Brigade in action under 40th Div Arty. We are Right Group consisting of four Batteries 174 (T/RHA and C)/183/covering Right Bde. 2nd (Centre) Division. Zone S27 a.00 – 32 8 C.5.2. Locations. HQ X13 b.1.1. 51°SE A/174 X16 a 6.9 (4 guns) X16 a 8.2 (2 guns) B/174 X11 d 8.8 (4 guns) 38 C.1.0 (2 guns) C/174 x 2.3 a. 5.9 (3 guns) 37 d 3.5.0.5 (2 guns), 32 a 9.1.7 1 gun D/174 X16 a 1.8 (4 hows) X17 G 1.9 (2 hows)
	1-8.5.18		Movement engaged by day, concentrations on Trench mortars frequently carried out and harassing fire maintained at night. Roving guns were employed to engage back areas -
	9.5.18	3.00am	Supported raid by 1st KRR's (99th Inf Bde) on post S27 d.15. Post found empty. (Harassing fire + concentrations carried out)
	(10.5.18) 11.5.18	4.30 pm 6.30 pm	Concentrated gas bombardment of X10 b and d, X11 C and d, + 17.0 carried out intermittently throughout the night, chiefly Yellow cross. Orgst. fire were afterwards on dugouts of D/174's detached section, and D/174's main position moved to X16 a. 9.5
	12.5.18	X1	D/174 detached section moved to X16 a. 9.5
	11-14.5.18		Harassing fire and concentrations carried out.
	14.5.18		C/181 relieved by A/186.
	18.5.18 22.5.18		C/174 Calibrates guns south. 16" Observation gunfire (16 Observation guns 3rd F.S.C. RE – 40th D.A. relieved by 32nd D.A.)
	14-26.5.18		A/174 Harassing fire and concentrations carried out (in conjunction with Lewis concentrations + T.M.s carried out + concentrations on T.M's carried out)
	24.5.18 26-31.5.18	10.00am	Harassing fire + concentrations on T.M.s carried out + concentrations on dugouts and B/174 is attached to us.
	30.5.18		On re-grouping A/176 leaves the group and B/174 is attached to us. Locations of Batteries A/174-X10 c 4.5.15 (4) × 16 a 78.26 (2). B/174-X11 d 77.76 (4) S14 a 01.99 (2) C/174-X 23 a 44.75 (3) S7A 34.08 (2) S20 B.1.7 (s); D/174-X. 16 d 64-97.7.7 (4), X23 B 46.80 (2); T/RHA-X16 a 5.5 (4) × 16 B 5.3.28 (2) B/174-X 22 B 58.69(4) × 17d 06.09 (2) – 15pn Anti-Tank gun S21 a.4.6

H.S. Maloney Lieut R.F.A.
for 174th Bde R.F.A.

WAR DIARY

INTELLIGENCE SUMMARY

174 Brigade R.F.A.

1st to 30th June, 1918.

Army Form C. 2118.

Place	Date	Hour	Summary of Events and Information	Remarks and references to Appendices
June	1	1.15 A.M.	2nd K.O.Y.L.I. raided enemy post at S.27.d.10.75 under cover of barrage provided by batteries of Right Group (174 Brigade R.F.A.). Raid was very successful - one prisoner being taken and the other four occupants of the post being killed. A proportion of the smoke shell was used in the barrage and the raiding troops reported that "the Artillery Barrage was clearly defined by the smoke".	France, B Sheet 51, 1/40,000. Right Group Operation Order No. 2 (attached as Appendix "A").
			Battery position of D/174 was intermittently shelled. Casualties - one Officer killed, two Officers wounded (one remained at duty).	
	2		Brigade in action as Right Group, Ixelles Division, VI Corps, covering Rifles Infantry	
	3		Brigade, Ixelles Division VI Corps. Battery Positions near HENDECOURT-LEZ-	France, Sheets 51 C & 51 B,
	4		RANSART. Other near RANSART and Wagon Lines at BELLACOURT.	1/40,000.
	5		Harassing fire and concentration day and night.	
	6			
	7	3.30 P.M.	Heavy artillery bombarded COURCELLES and GOMIECOURT. We co-operated by concentrating on HAMELINCOURT.	
	8			
	9		Harassing fire and concentrations.	
	10			

WAR DIARY

174 Brigade R.F.A.

INTELLIGENCE SUMMARY. 1st to 30th June, 1918.

Army Form C. 2118.

Place	Date	Hour	Summary of Events and Information	Remarks and references to Appendices
June	11	2 A.M.	Gas projected into HAMELIN COURT. Eighteen rounds batteries of Right Group. C. Hurdes by firing charges.	
	12		} Harassing fire and concentrations.	
	13			
	14			
	15			
	16			
	17	11.35 P.M.	2nd Oxford and Bucks L.I. (51st Brigade Right Division) raided enemy outposts in A2L. We raised the Left front, Right Division, in the artillery outposts. Operation unsuccessful.	France. Sheet 57c. 1/40.000
			Two actions per Battery of 174th Brigade relieved by corresponding Batteries of 155th Army Brigade, RFA. (night 17/18th).	
	18	6 P.M.	Wagon lines moved to FOSSEUX	LENS Sheet, 1/40,000, 3 G.8.1.
			3H.q./174 relieved by 3H.q./155. Remaining section per Battery of 174th Brigade relieved by corresponding Batteries of 155th Army Brigade, RFA. (night 18/4/18).	

174 Brigade R.F.A.

Army Form C. 2118.

WAR DIARY
INTELLIGENCE SUMMARY.
1st to 30th June, 1918.

(Erase heading not required.)

Place	Date	Hour	Summary of Events and Information	Remarks and references to Appendices
June	19		Brigade marched to PAS and FAMECHON, on transfer to IV Corps.	LENS Sheet, 1/100,000
	20		Hqrs. in PAS	
			Batteries in FAMECHON	
	21	9 P.M.	Brigade in Corps Reserve under orders of Left Division.	
	22		do. do. do. do. do.	
	23		Brigade in Mobile Reserve to Left Division.	
			do. do. do. do. do.	
	24		Relieves in Mobile Reserve by 26th Army Brigade, RFA.	France, Sheet 57D, 1/40,000
			Relieves fire Battery of 174th Brigade comprising Batteries of 310th Brigade, RFA ((62 D.A.) (night 24/25th).	
			15-pom Lines moved to C30d and J16a	
	25		Hqrs. 174 relieves Hqrs. 1310.	
			Hqrs. 174 relieves fire Battery of 174th Brigade relieves remaining Section per Battery of two Sections fire Battery of 310th Brigade, RFA (night 25/26th).	
			Hqrs. 174 now command Right group, Centre Division, IV Corps.	
			Right Infantry Brigade Centre Division, IV Corps.	
			Right group consists of A, B, C, D/174 and C, D/210 (42 D.A.)	
			Approximate front covered - K.17.00 to K.12a 75.40	

WAR DIARY

174 Brigade R.F.A.

INTELLIGENCE-SUMMARY.

1st to 30th June, 1918.

Army Form C. 2118.

Place	Date	Hour	Summary of Events and Information	Remarks and references to Appendices
June	25 (contd.)		Locations – Hdqrs 174	France Sheet 57 D, 1/40.000
			A/174 K1c 58.90	
			4 guns K7c 54.20	
			2 " K7d 73.70	
			B/174 4 " J5b 60.61 (silent)	
			2 " K2c 27.32	
			C/174 4 " J12a 70.63	
			2 " K8a 8.2	
			D/174 3 hows. J12d 00.15 (silent)	
			2 " K2c 83.28	
			1 how. K7d 31.29	
			B/174 15-pdr. Anti-Tank gun K3a 9.1	
	26		Section as above.	
	27		Heavy Artillery and Trench Mortars bombarded ROSSIGNOL WOOD (K12). We co-operated with bursts of fire throughout the day.	Right group Operation Order No. 6 (marked in Appendix "B").
		10.15 P.M.	Fighting patrols entered the wood, covered by our fire. Patrols ascertained that much damage to huts, strong points, dug-outs and trenches had been caused by the bombardment. Several dead germans were found in enemy trenches. Patrols inflicted further casualties on garrison of an enemy strong point which they encountered.	
	28 & 29		Harassing fire day and night.	
	30		Relief of 174th Brigade by 2nd Army Brigade N.Z.F.A. due to commence tonight.	

OC Capt. R.F.A.
p. Lieut-Col R.F.A.
Comdg. 174 Brigade R.F.A.

174 Brigade R.F.A.
War Diary - June, 1918.
Appendix "A".

RIGHT GROUP Operation Order No.2.

(cancels Right Group Operation No.2. of 30/5/18)

Ref. MOYENVILLE TRENCH MAP No.369 of 21/5/18.
1/20,000 Sheet 51^B S.W.

1. The K.O.Y.L.I. will carry out a raid on the enemy post S.27.d.10.75 on the night 31st/1st June.

2. <u>Zero hour</u> will be notified later.

3. <u>Position of assembly</u>
    Raiding party will be assembled at zero hour 150 yds. N.of N.E. corner of Bank S.27.b.2.0
    Covering party will be in the same position.

4. At <u>zero hour</u> raiding party crawl towards objective via Bank in S.27 central.
    zero plus 7   party rush post
    zero plus 12   party withdraw

5. <u>Artillery support</u>.

    <u>Zero to zero plus 7</u>

A/174	4 guns	bombard post		S.27.d.10.75
	2 "	"	"	S.27.d.05.68
T/RHA	2 "	"	"	S.27.d.10.75
	4 "	"	trench	S.27.c.70.68 to S.27.d.10.48
B/74			trench	S.27.c.28.00 to S.27.c.70.68
C/174			trench	S.27.d.10.48 to S.27.d.50.50
B/174			trench	S.27.d.43.59 to S.27.d.72.70
A/186	2 guns		trench	S.27.d.72.70 to S.27.d.89.69
	2 "		trench	S.27.d.72.50 to S.27.d.92.61
	2 "		trench	S.28.c.00.50 to S.28.c.21.28
D/174			M.G.	S.28.c.2.8
			"	S.28.c.21.28
			"	S.28.c.40.32
			"	S.28.c.52.40
			"	S.27.c.60.12
			trench	A.3.b.40.56

    <u>Rate of fire</u>

    18-pdrs   A/174)
) - 4 rds. per gun per min.
              T/RHA)

    Remainder - 2 "   "   "   "   "

    4.5"hows. - 1 rd. "   "   "   "

    <u>Zero plus 7 to zero plus 15</u>

A/174	4 guns	trench	S.27.d.03.50 to S.27.d.21.28
	2 "	trench	S.27.c.58.36 to S.27.c.70.68
T/RHA		trench	S.27.c.70.68 to S.27.d.10.48 but switch to right where necessary to give clearance of 150 yds. between line of fire and post S.27.d.10.75

-2-

Zero plus 7 to zero plus 15 (contd)

    B/74   trench S.27.c.28.00 to S.27.c.58.36

    C/174   trench S.27.d.21.28 to S.27.d.32.20
                                   to S.27.d.52.33

    B/174)
    A/186) - NO CHANGE
    D/174)

Rates of fire

        18-pdrs. 3 rds. per gun per min.
        4.5" hows. 2 "   "   "   "   "

6. Ammunition 18-pdrs

    T/RHA and A/174   all shrapnel

    2 guns A/186 on S.28.c.00.50 to S.28.c.21.28   all H.E.

    Remainder   75% shrapnel   25% H.E.

    Corrector to give 50% on graze.

Smoke shell

    All Batteries RIGHT GROUP will fire smoke shell as under :

    C/174) 1 rd. smoke per 50 yds front per 2 mins.
    B/174) from zero to zero plus 15.

    A/186   1 rd. smoke per 2 mins for 2 guns
             S.27.d.72.70 to S.27.d.89.69

    A/174) 1 rd. smoke per 50 yds smoke per 2 mins.
    T/RHA) from zero plus 7 to zero plus 15.

7. Watches will be synchronised at H.Q. RIGHT GROUP at 7 p.m. An Officer per Battery will be present at that hour.

8. All doubtful ammunition will be carefully excluded.

9. A special Meteor has been asked for at 12 midnight.

10. In case of S.O.S. guns will immediately get back on S.O.S. lines.

11. ACKNOWLEDGE.

31/5/18.

                                                       Lieut.-Col., R.F.A.,
                                                       Cmdg. RIGHT GROUP.

SECRET

RIGHT GROUP - 57th D.A.

174 Brigade R.F.A.
War Diary - June 1918.
Appendix "B".

Operation Order No.6 - 26/6/18.

Ref: Sheet 1/20,000 57^D N.E. ~~Trenches corrected to 20/5/18.~~ *Edition 5d local*

1. On June 27th the Field Artillery will co-operate with the Heavy Artillery in a bombardment of ROSSIGNOL WOOD.

2. All posts forward of the line COD TRENCH - TANK TRENCH - HIGH ST - HERRING TRENCH will be cleared before 9 a.m. and will be re-occupied from 9.30 p.m.

3. At 10.15 p.m. fighting patrol will enter ROSSIGNOL WOOD by the sap leaving Railway trench at K.12.b.37.70 K.12.b.50.57 K.12.b.62.52 and proceed down this sap as far as possible. They will withdraw after 30 minutes.

4. Right Group Tasks as under - all active 18-pdrs and 4.5" hows :-

    (a)   12.15 p.m. to 12.20 p.m.)   Group area - Portion of wood
           1.29 p.m. -" 1.34 p.m.)   K.12.b.02.30 - K.12.b.67.30 -
           1.38 p.m. - 1.43 p.m.)   K.12.b.79.20 - K.12.d.42.81 -
           1.55 p.m. - 2.0 p.m.)   K.12.a.92.15 - K.12.b.02.30
           5.10 p.m. - 5.15 p.m.)
           6.15 p.m. - 6.20 p.m.)   Within the above area boundaries
           6.31 p.m. - 6.36 p.m.)   between 18-pdr Batteries are as
           6.56 p.m. - 7.1 p.m.)   under :-
           7.8 p.m. - 7.13 p.m.)
           7.25 p.m. - 7.30 p.m.)

    C/174   E. boundary to trench K.12.b.18.00 - K.12.b.32.30

    C/210   thence to trench K.12.d. 32.96 - K.12.b.50.31

    A/174   remainder of zone
                S. of trench K.12.b.47.28 - K.12.b.68.30

    B/174   remainder of zone North of trench
                K.12.b.47.28 - K.12.b.68.30

    D/174   W. of trench K.12.d.32.96 - K.12.b.50.31

    D/210   E. of trench   -do-   -do-

18-pdrs will search and sweep the areas.
4.5" hows. will fire on selected trench junctions and works.

Rate of fire - Intense.

    (b) 9.30 p.m. - 9.35 p.m.) C/174) Trench K.12.a.96.12 to
          9.42 p.m. - 9.47 p.m.) C/210) K.12.d.50.82
          9.55 p.m. - 10.0 p.m.) A/174 K.12.d.50.82 - K.12.d.50.50
         10.10 p.m. - 10.15 p.m.) B/174 K.12.d.50.50 - K.12.d.59.35
)
                                D/210 C.T.S. leading into wood from
                                       L.7.c.29.48
                                       L.7.c.12.48
                                     K.12.d.69.34

                              D/174 C.T.S. leading into wood from
                                       K.12.c.91.60

        4.5" hows: to pay particular attention to trench junctions

Rate of fire - intense

(c) 10.15 p.m. to 11.15 p.m. ~~Below~~ C/174 will not fire

Targets as for (b). Bursts of harassing fire at rapid rate will be fired

10.25 p.m. to 10.29 p.m.
10.39 p.m. - 10.43 p.m.
10.56 p.m. - 11.2 p.m.
11.12 p.m. - 11.15 p.m.

No guns to fire within Safety limit of line K12b 20.43 K12b 36.35 K12b 45.23

5. Section B/174 will stand by from 9.a.m. to dusk to take on fleeting opportunities.
F.O.O.s at X O.P.s will keep a sharp look-out for movement at ROSSIGNOL WOOD and engage it with section B/174.

6. A sharp look-out must be kept for S.O.S. during the period our trenches are vacated.

7. Watches will be synchronised at 8.30 a.m. and 8.0 p.m.

8. ACKNOWLEDGE.

26/6/18.

Captain, R.F.A.,
Adjutant, RIGHT GROUP.

Distribution :-

A,B,C,D/174,
C,D/210,

174th Brigade R.F.A.

WAR DIARY or INTELLIGENCE SUMMARY
(Erase heading not required.)

Army Form C. 2118.

1–31 July 1918.

Place	Date	Hour	Summary of Events and Information	Remarks and references to Appendices
	1/7/18		HQ W.L. moved to PAS. Relief of remaining section for Battery completed	
	2/7/18	8 A.M.	High 1/2 A.D. Batteries withdrawn to W.L.s.	
	3/7/18		A/Q/174 relieved by 14dge/2nd Army Bde N.Z.F.A. Brigade entrained at DOULLENS and MONDICOURT (LENS Sheet). Commenced journey back to Flanders.	
	4/7/18		Brigade detrained at PROVEN and travelled by WILLS in and around DROGLANDT. One section for Battery placed in positions to cover the EAST POPERINGHE System (3rd R Division Section, II Corps Sector) Front Covered. A22 & 35.05 to G.H.C. 70.00. (Sheet 26) A/174. F.28 & 9.3. B/174 F.28 & 4.3. C/174. F.28 & 9.95 D/174 F.29 & 55.70 (Sheet 27)	
	5-7/7/18		Batteries carried out training Schemes.	
	8/7/18		No change in locations	
			174 R Bde (less one section in positions as above). Placed at disposal of XIX Corps. In case of tactical necessity.	
	9–12/7/18		No change in locations. Battery training continued.	
	13/7/18		174th R Bde R.F.A. & 39 R.F.A.C Horse Show or Sports held at DROGLANDT.	
	14–21/7/18		Battery training continued.	
	22/7/18		" " " Bde ceased to be at disposal of XIX Corps.	
	23–29/7/18		" " "	
	30/7/18		174 Bde R.F.A. Orders & relieve 186 Bde R.F.A. in the line. Relief of forward section and one section for Battery completed.	Sheet 28.
	31/7/18		1/31/18 Bde R.F.A. relieved 186/186 Bde R.F.A. — section for Battery in forward positions withdrawn. Relief of Bde R.F.A. Section for Battery of 186 Bde completed. Bre tactically controlled by 33 R.A A/174. H.4.C.1.1. B/174. H.11.C.80.33. C/174. H.10.a.6.8. D/174. H.12.d.4.26.	

C/174. H.2.b.90.25 (AMERSTINGHE) (H.4.T.455)

Comdg. 174 Brigade R.F.A.

CMMullen? Bjr. for Lieut-Col. R.F.A.

WAR DIARY
INTELLIGENCE SUMMARY

1 – 31 August 1918.
174th Brigade, R.F.A

Army Form C. 2118.

Place	Date	Hour	Summary of Events and Information	Remarks and references to Appendices
	1/8/18		Wagon lines moved to vicinity of ST SIXTE.	Ref Sheet 27
	2/8/18		Harassing fire carried out.	
	3/8/18		Batteries came out of action (not relieved) – withdrew to wagon lines.	
	4/8/18		HQ and Batteries moved by forced march to billets in DEGRANDT area.	
	5/8/18		Bde moved by forced march to billets in WARDRECQUES. Via WINNEZEELE – CASSEL – RENESCURE.	Ref Hap (Hazebrouck S.)
	6/8/18		Held at G.H.Q reserve.	
	13/8/18 to 14/8/18		Battery training. Tactical Schemes carried out. Move on resume position under orders of 29. Bn Arty, dismtd, looking batteries from each battery.	Ref Sheet 27
	14/8/18		Brigade moved to vicinity of WALLON-CAPPELL. HQ at U.17.b.5.7. A/174 U.17.b.5.7. B/174 U.18.a.9.5. C/174. V.20.a.7.9. D/174. Y.13.c.8.7. T.M.I. Section 39 BAC. Came under Orders of 174 Std R.T.M.	
	15/8/18		Bde moved into action under orders of 29th Bn Arty at 12 midnight. Positions as follows:– HQ W.16.a.5.9. A/174 W.24.a.8.2. B/174 W.24 to 0.5. C/174 W.24.b.4.8. D/174 W.18.a.05.70. Batteries registered Suvae.	
	16/8/18			
	17/8/18			
	18/8/18		Attack Lunaep carried on in support of Offensive Operation carried out by 9th and 29th Divisions. Attack was successful. Lines advanced to ALBERT CROSSING – F.8.c Central – F.d.a. Central – F.3. Central – three to original line. X.28.a.30.00; X.28.b.0.8. – X.22.a.5.3 – three to original line. Harassing fire carried out during the night.	Ref Sheet 27 + 36.A
	19/8/18		Attack barrage fired in support of minor Operation by 29th Bn on our front, by 31st Bn on our right flank. Lines advanced to COURRIER COTTAGE – L'ABBE Farm – Railway Crossing F.8.C.8.6.	
	21/8/18		Half Bde moved to vicinity of BOIRE. HQ/174. Y.24.b.5.5. A/174. Y.24.b.4.3. B/174. Y.13.c.5.9. C/174. Y.18.a.08. D/17. Y.19.a.7.4. Batteries established in action under orders of 29 Bn Arty to harass lines as above.	

WAR DIARY
or
INTELLIGENCE SUMMARY.
(Erase heading not required.)

Army Form C. 2118.

Place	Date	Hour	Summary of Events and Information	Remarks and references to Appendices
	22/8/18		Brigade Entrained at St. OMER — Commenced Journey to First Army Area	Ref Sheet 51.B.
	23/8/18		Brigade detrained at SAVY and marched to Bullet h' ACQ.	
			Order of 2nd Canadian D.A. 39th Div Arty came under	
	24/8/18		Bde moved to hqrs lines near the CITADEL in ARRAS. Guns placed in position as under. HQ. G.35.a.0.4.	Ref Sheet G.35.c.25.15
			and Gun lines personnel of Batteries. Also a Guard withdrawn to W.L.S. A/174. M.S.a.36.85. B/174. M.S.a.36.85. C/174. G.35.c.25.15	
	25/8/18		Battery positions manned	
	26/8/18	3.am	Guns in support of attack by the Canadian Corps. — Bde advanced, taking up positions as follows	
			HQ C/174. N.3.d.2.3. A/174. N.11.b.7.4. B/174. N.11.d.8.5. C/174. N.w.c.1.8. D/174. N.11.a.8.2. Wagon lines horses	
	27/8/18	10 am	Batteries fires in support of continued attack on enemy by Canadian Corps and further advanced to	
			positions as follows in vicinity of GUÉMAPPE. HQ. O.13.b.2.3. A/174. O.13.d.8.9. B/174. O.13.d.8.2.	
			C/174. O.13.b.7.5. D/174. O.13.d.2.9. Wagon lines moved up to N.11.	
	28/8/18	12.30p.	Attack Barrage. No change in locations	
			Wagon lines moved up to N.17. a.c.4.	
	29/8/18		Supported attack by 2nd Canadian Inf. Bde. on OLIVE TR. & CABLE TR to O.29. & O.30.	Ref Sheet 51.B SW
	31/8/18	5 am	Bde advanced, taking up positions as follows in the vicinity of CHERISY. HQ. O.21.d.45.15.	
		12 noon	A/174. O.28.a.4.4. B/174. O.27.b.65.20. C/174. O.28.a.15.26. D/174. O.28.a.33.80.	
			Wagon lines to O.19.	

P.H. Wilkins Lt. Col. Lieut-Col. R.F.A.
Comdg 174 Brigade R.F.A.

17th Brigade R.A.

WAR DIARY covering period 1-30/9/1918.

INTELLIGENCE SUMMARY.

VOL 31

Place	Date	Hour	Summary of Events and Information	Remarks and references to Appendices
Nr CHERISY	1/9/18	4.50am	Batteries fired a barrage in support of minor operation carried out by 2nd Canadian Infantry Div. to establish new advanced line.	Ref. Hole Sheet 51B S.E.
		11.35p	Enemy harassed troops along road P.31.d.0.4 to P.22.a.0.0. for 20 minutes - Enemy gun of 5.9mm.	
	2/9/18	5 am	Supports attack by 2nd Canadian Inf. Div. on Cahary Drocourt Queant (2nd objective famis)	
		9 am	Role stood by ready to advance - being in Corps Reserve.	
		9 p	Batteries moved forward & took up positions as follows:- Bde HQ V.18.5.7. A/17 V.id 65.90. B/17 V.16.6.4. C/17 V.16.55.60. D/17 V.1.d.5.6. Infr lines h. 0.27.b.t.d and 0.28.a.t.c.	
	3/9/18	2 p	Batteries advanced, taking up positions as follows - HQ/17 V.11.a 85.00. A/17 V.12.a 37.22. B/17 Y.12.a 3.4. C/17 V.10.b 15.25. D/17 Y.10.b. 3.3. Infantry lines at V.10.a.b and V.9.a.b. all Batteries carried out harassing fire during the night.	
	4/9/18	9 am	Batteries registered & fired on fleeting targets.	
		6.30p	C/17 moved forward and took up position at W.13.a.15.45.	
	5/9/18		17th Bde R.F.A. became left side of Left Group (29 Div Arty) covering 6th C.I.B.	
	6/9/18		Infantry lines moved back to positions as follows M/17 P.32.c Central B/17 P.32.d Central C/17 P.33.a	
	7/9/18		D/17 V.16.5.0.	
	8/9/18		Harassing fire carried out. Batteries moved to locations as follows. MAIN POSITIONS:- A/17 Y.12.a 30.06 #4.6mo FORWARD POSITIONS W.1.c 70.10 2 guns B/17 Y.12.a 28.29 do W.1.c 5.42 do C/17 W.13.a 11.20 do W.1.c 40.60 d D/17 N.6/15.9+ 3do W.7.c 45.65 do D/17 Shelling Guns at W.1.C.15.	

174th Brigade RFA

WAR DIARY
or
INTELLIGENCE SUMMARY
(Erase heading not required.)

Army Form C. 2118.

Instructions regarding War Diaries and Intelligence Summaries are contained in F. S. Regs., Part II. and the Staff Manual respectively. Title pages will be prepared in manuscript.

Place	Date	Hour	Summary of Events and Information	Remarks and references to Appendices
	9/9/18		No change in locating Hygun bg carries out.	
	10/9/18		Major Lines move to positions as follows. HQ 174 CHATEAU HENDECOURT A17d U5d 6.8. B/174 V13.1.7	Ref Sheet 51.B.SE
			C/174 V3.a.2.2. B/174 V.2.a.1.1.	
	12/9/18	1.am	Left took part in Gas bombardment of enemy battery positions and forward areas.	
	13-14/9/18		Harassing fire carried out.	
	15/9/16		C/174 moved to position at V.10.b.92.27.	
	17/9/18		Lets HQ moved to V.9.a.1.1. B/174 moved to same to (man & shell) position in V.11.c.41.74	
			Two forward section moved back to positions in V.12.a.76.29. Major Lines moved & position as under:- B/174 U5d 3.6. C/174 U6a.3.1. D/174 U.12.d.3.5.	
			C/174 forward section moved back to position in Y.12.a.28.39.	
	20/9/18		Bty forward sections re adjusted as follows:- 51 gun A/174 +1 gun C/174 at W1C.7.1. under officer of C/174 at V.12.a.25.40. -do- C/52.	
			Harassing fire carried on during the night. 51 gun B/174 +1 gun C/52 at V.12.a.25.40. -do- C/52.	
	21/9/18		-do- -do- Ammunition taken up to forward battle positions - pack animals used.	
	24/9/18		-do- Ammunition taken up to forward battle positions as follows - A/174 W136.97.37.	
	25/9/18	9.p	3 gun per battery moved into forward battle position as follows - D/174 W13f.85.74 MQ174 W13.f.52.90.	
			B/174 W13.b.60.06. C/174 W13f.75.25	
	26/9/18	10b	3 remaining gun per battery moved into forward battle positions.	
	27/9/18	5.20am	Zero hour - Batteries fire in support of attack carried out by 1st Can Div.	
		9b	Battery ordered to advance & take up position of assembly in W.23d.	
			Reste Commanders sent forward & reconnoitre fire and teleph...	

WAR DIARY
INTELLIGENCE SUMMARY

Army Form C. 2118.

174 Brigade R.F.A.

Place	Date	Hour	Summary of Events and Information	Remarks and references to Appendices
	27/9/18	4.30 pm	Batteries came into position of assembly in W.2.9.6.	
		7 pm	Batteries moved into positions in W.2.a & c. Bde H.Q. at W.2.d. 25.30.	Inform lines
	28/9/18	7.30 am	Mounted patrols went out to find our situation	
		7.30 am	Bde Commander went forward & reconnoitred.	
		9 am	Batteries moved forward into a position of assembly in X.8.c-d	
		9.30 am	— arrived at position of assembly as ordered.	
		12 noon	Batteries moved forward to positions as under. H.Q.174 X.3.c.17. M/174 X.3.c.2.4. B/174 X.2.d.7.5. C/174 X.3.a.0.2. D/174 X.2.c.6.6.	
			Sage Lines in X.8.c.d.	
	29/9/18	at	Fired at S.O.S. lines. Harassing fire down the night	
	30/9/18	8 am	Fires in support of minor attack. Harassing fire carried out	
			Batteries engaged to Enemy Enemy movement throughout the day. Harassing fire during the night. 11,120 rds Ammunition fired. Batteries of 174 Brigade R.F.A. between 5 am 30/9/18 and 5 am 1/10/18.	

Arthur Capt.
Lieut-Col. R.F.A.
Comdg. 174 Brigade R.F.A.

174 Bde R.F.A.
1st to 31st October 1918.

WAR DIARY or INTELLIGENCE SUMMARY
Army Form C. 2118.

174 Brigade R.F.A.

Place	Date	Hour	Summary of Events and Information	Remarks and references to Appendices
	1/10/18	05.30	Barrage supplied in support of minor Operation.	Ref: Sheet 51-B Hoegeen
			Enemy heavy bombardment during the day.	
		19.15	First rounds Preparation.	
		20.15	All Batteries firing on Harassing fire.	
	2/10/18		Enemy bombardment Subsided throughout the day.	
		23.50–01.24	Supported minor operations carried out by 11th Div. Enters line to re-establish line.	
		18.35–19.05	Fired Counter Preparation.	
	3/10/18 01.01–01.21	Sulphur Barrage in support of Operations by 11th Div.	
			Map Lines moved 3 Batteries as follows – A/174. W.11.a.6.3. A/174. W.11.d.5.5. B/174. W.10.a.3.7. C/174. W.11.d.8.2.	
	4/10/18	18.00	Change of Zone – Wiring 2 new C.F.A.	
		19.00	Bdy H.Q. moved to new M.Q. at X.13.d 65.90.	
	5/10/18	18.00	1 Section of Battery moved to W.line 13.a & d. C.F.A. 1 Section of 15th Bde C.F.A. took over corresponding battery positions. Ammunition handed + taken over.	Gunline Ref Sheet 51.B
			Relief of 13 A. C.F.A. completed. Locations as follows –	W.29.d.8.8.
			HQ/174. F.10.a.50.60.	W.29.a.50.70.
			A/174. F.10.a.00.50.	W.30.b.3.8.
			B/174. F.4.a.80.30.	W.29.b.2.5.
			C/174. F.8.d.85.75.	W.24.d.O.O.
			D/174. F.3.c.15.15.	
	6/10/18			
	7/10/18	18.00	C/174. moved position forward to F.5.b.70.50. (5 guns). A.1.b.20.70. (1 gun) D/174. moved position to F.12.a.80.20. (4 guns) to A.1.a.05.20. (2 guns) B/174. moved 1 gun to position with C/174 & single guns, halting a composite Section under an A/174. forward Section to A.1.b.15.10. Harassing fire carried out on approaches to CAMBRAI.	
		19.00		

WAR DIARY or INTELLIGENCE SUMMARY

171 Brigade R.F.A.
1st to 31st October 1918
Army Form C. 2118.

Date	Hour	Summary of Events and Information	Remarks and references to Appendices
8/10/18	04.30	All Batteries took part in bombarding areas as follows – A+B.15.80. – A+a.95.98 – A+a.75.95. A.4.4.51.72 – A.4.4.70.35. – A+b.10.48. – A+b.15.80. 750 rds per Battery fired.	Sheet 51 A. 1/40.000
		Harrassing enemy movement during the day.	
		A/171. Hd Qrs. A8 b.6. B/171. Hd Qrs. A8 c.6.u.	
9/10/18	09.00	Moved to position of assembly h. S.28.6.	
	18.30	Hd Qrs in action as follows – Hd Qrs T.2.c.0.4. A/171. T.2.d.3½. B/171. T.2.c.4.0. C/171. T.2.c.50.20. D/171. T.2.c.50.10.	
10/10/18	09.00	Fire Barrage in Support of attack.	
	12.00	Moved forward to positions of assembly as follows – A/171. T.17.a.40.30. B/171. T.17.a.40.30. M/171. T.18.d.10.50. C/171. T.18.d.25.80. D/171. T.18.d.50.55. A/171. T.16.c.8.5. B/171. T.16.d Central B/171. T.18.a.55.50. D/171. T.22.b.4.4. C/171. T.16.d.2.4. D/171. T.22.a.8.9. Ayu Lines Hd Qrs. Avesnes Le Sec.	
11/10/18	09.00	Fire Barrage in Support of attack of 57th Bde on V7.a. & d.	In Ayr Lines 0.32. G.1.6.
	15.00	Moved to positions of assembly at V7.a. & d. Took up position as under – Hd Qrs. On Padure. M/171. 0.26.d.0.0. B/171. 0.26.c.0.6. C/171. 0.19.d.7.1. D/171. 0.19.d.9.2.	0.30.
12/10/18	09.00	Fire Barrage in Support of attack & covering 152 Bde 51st Division.	
	11.00	Hd Qrs Hd Qrs position h. U.3.a.10.4.	
	18.20	C/171. Hd Qrs position h. U.3.a.4.4.	

174 Brigade R.F.A.

WAR DIARY or INTELLIGENCE SUMMARY

In the Field. October 1918. Army Form C. 2118.

Place	Date	Hour	Summary of Events and Information	Remarks and references to Appendices
	13/14/18	18.50	Bgrs. moved & positions in U.4.a.4.4.	M. Sheet 51. A
		15.00	Wagon Lines moved back to positions as follows –	
	14/15/18	08.10.	A/174. U.7.c.4.6. B/174. U.7.c.4.6. C/174. U.7.c. 7.6.	
			B/174. U.13.a. 0.5.	
		16.30.	Four cannons on Railway O.10.c and O.9.b in support of fighting patrols reconnoitring	
			enemy forward posts.	
			A/174 held section in readiness however as at Bastion & lake on any enemy tanks.	
		17.30.	B/174. moved up to a forward section to O.29.c.7.3. Kaifelde Railway.	
			Battery wagon lines moved to area T.18. V.13.	
	16/17/18	15.00	M/174. moved their position to V.3.a. 25.15. leaving only Anti-tank section forward.	
			D/174. moved section forward to O.30.c. 8.3.	
	19/19/18	14.00	A/174. Withdrew their forward section to main position at V.3.a. 25.15.	
	20/10/18	16.30.	Batteries moved forward & positions as under –	
			Gun Positions. Wagon Lines.
			A/174. O.10.c. 3.2. V.3.a. 25.15.
			B/174. O.10.b. 3.1. U.4.a. 4.4.
			C/174. O.10.b. 2.4. V.3.a. 0.4.
			D/174. O.10.c. 3.8. V.3.a. 2.4.
			O.4.d.6.0.
	21/10/18	14.00.	All moved forward & positions as under –	
			Gun Positions. Wagon Lines.
			Bn. HQ. I. 15. a. 1.6. Wagon Lines.
			A/174. I.31.b.7.05.75 I.35.c. Central.
			B/174. I.31.b. 1.1. I.36. a. 5.8.
			C/174. I.31.b. 1.1. I.36. a. 5.8.
			D/174. I.31.b. 8.0 I.35.d. 1.9.

17A Brigade R.F.A.   WAR DIARY or INTELLIGENCE SUMMARY

Army Form C. 2118.

1st to 31st October 1918.

(Erase heading not required.)

Instructions regarding War Diaries and Intelligence Summaries are contained in F. S. Regs., Part II. and the Staff Manual respectively. Title pages will be prepared in manuscript.

Place	Date	Hour	Summary of Events and Information	Remarks and references to Appendices
	22/10/18	09.00	Fired Chinese Barrage.	Sheet 51A. 1/40,000
		11.30.	— do —	
		16.00	— do —	
		16.30.	Forward battle position of Bde HQrs established at J.25.a.4.4.	
	23/10/18	03.00	Fired Chinese Barrage.	
		15.00	— do —	
		15.45	Attack by 51st Div. on MAING.	
	24/10/18	04.00	Supporting Barrage to support this attack. — Batteries remained in action after completion of Barrage.	
		09.00	3 Coy. Battery of Artillery across ESCAILLON River.	
	25/10/18	17.30.	Bde H.Q. withdrew to NOYELLES.	
		16.55.	Bde batteries from action into Corps Reserve — Billets at NOYELLES.	
			A/17th J.35.a.1.5.	
			11/17th. J.35.c.5.5.	
			B/17th. J.35.a.1.9.	
			C/17th. J.35.a.5.3.	
			D/17th. J.22.c.8.3.	
	26.10.18		Corps Reserve	
	27.10.18		" do "	
	28.10.18	12.00	Positions reconnoitred by M+G. for attack on morning of 30th.	
	29.10.18		attack postponed 24 hours.	
	30.10.18		Guns went into action and Crewed S.O.S. lines. attack postponed 24 hours. Ate M+G remained at NOYELLES.	

J B Oberg?
Lt. Col. RFA
Comdg. 17th Bde RFA

14		174th Brigade R.F.A. November 1918.	Army Form C. 2118.

WAR DIARY or **INTELLIGENCE SUMMARY**

Place	Date	Hour	Summary of Events and Information	Remarks and references to Appendices
	31/10/18.	15.00	Bde HQ. moved to stable position near MAING	
	1/11/18.	05.15	Supported attack by 4th Canadian Division - all objectives have taken. Batteries remained in position after barrage - covering S.O.S. lines.	
	2/11/18.		Further progress in VALENCIENNES, and on Canadian front, our guns unchanged, and remained in position. Not crossing army zone - but awaiting orders.	
	3/11/18.		In action - awaiting orders.	
	3/11/18.	16.00	HQ. moved into MAING	
	4/11/18.	07.00	Brigade moved to St. Amand area by march route and arrived in COUTICHES area at 17.00 hrs Batteries and Bde HQ. in billets as follows locations:-	
			Bde HQ. R. 4. b. 6.2. A/174. R. 4. d. 4.7. } LA PICTERIE. B/174. R. 4. b. 6.3. C/174. R. 2. b. 6.5. D/174. R. 3. b. 8.8. } FAUMONT.	
	5/11/18 to 30/11/18		Battery & Brigade training carries out, also Educational Lectures given to all ranks. Assistance given to French farmers viz- 50 horses loaned to farm work daily to plough.	

A.M. Kino Major R.A.
Comdg 174th Brigade R.F.A.

17th Brigade R.M.A. WAR DIARY or INTELLIGENCE SUMMARY.

Army Form C. 2118.

November 1918.

Place	Date	Hour	Summary of Events and Information	Remarks and references to Appendices
	1/12/18		Brigade still in 8th Corps Area — Costumes and Equipment Bde. H.Q. & Batteries billets as follows, location:	
			Bde. H.Q. R.4.b.4.7. A/174. R.4.d.4.7. B/174. R.4.b.6.3. Sheet 44 A C/174. R.2.b.6.5. " Givry D/174. R.3.b.7.8.	
	3/12/18		Saddling & Riding Instruction carried out. Educational Lectures given to all ranks in the different Batteries. to Brand Avenue, say 25 horses assisted from day to day in 16. transport duty in Costumes & Gueuts on Demande.	J.R. &c.

(4)

WO95/2574
Mar'16 - Jan'17
179 Bde RFA

39TH DIVISION
DIVL ARTILLERY

179TH BRIGADE R.F.A.

MAR 1916-JAN 1917

To 5 ARMY

39th Divisional Artillery.

Disembarked HAVRE 5th March 1916.

179th BRIGADE

ROYAL FIELD ARTILLERY.

MARCH 1916
/
Jan 1917

179 RFA
Vol 2
vol 1 of 2

XXXIX

CONFIDENTIAL

War Diary.
of
179th Bde. R.F.A.

From March 4th 1916 to March 31st 1916.

(Volume 1)

Army Form C. 2118

WAR DIARY
INTELLIGENCE SUMMARY
(Erase heading not required.)

Instructions regarding War Diaries and Intelligence Summaries are contained in F.S. Regs., Part II. and the Staff Manual respectively. Title Pages will be prepared in manuscript.

Place	Date	Hour	Summary of Events and Information	Remarks and references to Appendices
Milford Surrey.	4/3/16		The Brigade left Witley Camp and entrained for Southampton Headquarters being the last to leave at 3.10 P.M. B. Battery and Bde Ammunition Column crossed the Channel on , Hdqrs, A, C & D, batteries crossed on 'AFRICAN PRINCE' leaving Southampton 8.10 P.M. The passage was good and nothing unusual occurred.	
France	5/3/16		Le Havre was reached on Sunday morning and disembarkation commenced at 11.15 A.M. Hdqrs went to DOCKS REST CAMP arriving there 5.30 P.M. The batteries went to different camps.	
Havre BLARINGHEM	6/3/16 7/3/16		Brigade left Havre and entrained for BLARINGHEM. Hdqrs and some batteries detraining at THIENNES and remainder at STEENBECQUE. The whole country was covered with snow and no some batteries and the B.A.C. arrived after dark difficulty was experienced in getting vehicles parked and horses tied up.	During journey a man of B. Bty fell out of train; being killed and other injured necessitating his going to hospital
	8/to 10/3/16		Brigade remained at BLARING & HEM.	

WAR DIARY

INTELLIGENCE SUMMARY

(Erase heading not required.)

Army Form C. 2118

Instructions regarding War Diaries and Intelligence Summaries are contained in F. S. Regs., Part II. and the Staff Manual respectively. Title Pages will be prepared in manuscript.

Place	Date	Hour	Summary of Events and Information	Remarks and references to Appendices
	10/3/16	(a.m.)	Brigade left BLARINGHEM at 8. A.M. Q: party of 1 Officer, 1 QMS, 1 Sgt and 1 Rank and file from each unit under 2/Lieut C.W. LONGLEY going on ahead as billetting party, declaration being ESTAIRES. The route taken was via BOESEGHEM — STEENBECQUE — STEENBECQUE STATION — LA RUE DES MORTS — NEUF BERQUIN — ESTAIRES. Bde arrived ESTAIRES about 4.0 P.M. Weather very cold and damp. Billets were in NEUF-BERQUIN ROAD.	
ESTAIRES	11/3/16	(a.m.) 3 PM 6 PM	In morning C.O. and Bty Commanders visited positions to be taken up by units. A/Bty⁰ left for FLEURBAIX. B/Bty⁰ left for various positions. Ref/Map. BELGIUM and PART OF FRANCE Sheet No 36 N.W. Unit references:— A Bty H 31 a 3.1 B do H 32 a 9.4 C do H 26 d 6.4 D do H 33 b 1.9 Am Col G 26 a 1.1 The Bde was attached to 8ᵗʰ DIVISION for instructional purposes, A & B Btys C & D Btys being attached to LEFT GROUP under Col NEVINSON and A & B 15ᵗʰ to CENTRE GROUP under Col BUTLER.	

WAR DIARY
or
INTELLIGENCE SUMMARY

(Erase heading not required.)

Army Form C. 2118

Place	Date	Hour	Summary of Events and Information	Remarks and references to Appendices
FLEURBAIX	12/3/16		Occupied by Batteries in repairing and strengthening gun positions. A few 4.2 shells fell in FLEURBAIX between 5 and 6 P.M.	
	13/3/16 to 23/3/16		Batteries carried out registrations.	
	24/3/16	6.0 P.M.	Batteries went out of action and returned to Wagon lines positions:— Ref Map. BELGIUM and PARTS OF FRANCE Sheet 36 N.W. 1/40000 A. Battery B. do C. do D. do	
	25/3/16		Brigade left 8th Divisional area at 9.30 a.m. (The kindness and thoughtful action shown to this Bde by General Nicholson and Royal Artillery of the 8th Div during attachment was very much noted and greatly appreciated). The Route taken to new Area was via ESTAIRES – MERVILLE – ROBECQ – BUSNES – BERGUETTE. C Battery was left behind awaiting orders from 19th Div. Bde arrived new area at 5.0 P.M. Weather good.	
BERGUETTE	26/3/16		Weather wet in morning up to 9.0 a.m. then good. Positions of units:— A Bty O.16 a.4.6 A Bty O.16 d.8.3 Hdqrs O.16 c.8.6 B Bty O.23 b.3.4 Amm Col O.22 d.0.4 C Bty R.33 b.5.6 Ref Map FRANCE Sheet 36a	

Army Form C. 2118

WAR DIARY
or
INTELLIGENCE SUMMARY
(Erase heading not required.)

Instructions regarding War Diaries and Intelligence Summaries are contained in F. S. Regs., Part II. and the Staff Manual respectively. Title Pages will be prepared in manuscript.

Place	Date	Hour	Summary of Events and Information	Remarks and references to Appendices
BERGUETTE	27/3/16		Weather Fair.	
do	28/3/16		Weather cold and windy but dry. Field day under Brigade arrangements, starting 9.0 a.m finish 2.0 P.M.	
do	29/3/16		Weather cold but dry. Training under Unit arrangements.	
do	30/3/16		Weather very good. do	
do	31/3/16		do do	

A. H. Kennard
Lt. Col. R.F.A.
Officer Comdg 179th Bde. R.F.A.

39th Divisional Artillery.

179th BRIGADE

ROYAL FIELD ARTILLERY

APRIL 1916

INTELLIGENCE SUMMARY

(Erase heading not required.)

Instructions regarding War Diaries and Intelligence Summaries are contained in F.S. Regs., Part II. and the Staff Manual respectively. Title Pages will be prepared in manuscript.

Place	Date	Hour	Summary of Events and Information	Remarks and references to Appendices
BERGUETTE	1/4/16		Weather very good. Inspection and march past by Gen MERCER. Dismounted parade in afternoon for Brig-Gen GILLSON. On both occasions Inspecting Generals pleased with him out.	See 1
do	2/4/16		Weather good. Party left at 8.45 in accordance with D.A. orders. Brigade training.	
do	3/4/16		do.	
do	4/4/16		Weather fair. Training under unit arrangements. Adjutant and 5 Telephonists went up to 33rd Div for instruction. Training under unit arrangements.	
do	5/4/16		do.	
do	6/4/16		do.	
do	7/4/16		Training under unit arrangements. Col KENNARD went up to front. Capt BELL in charge of Bde. Training under unit arrangements.	
do	8/4/16		do.	
do	9/4/16		do. G.O.C. R.A. Inspected Billets and Lines.	
do	10/4/16		Inspection at 4.0 P.M. by G.O.C. 1st Army. Party that left on 2/4/16 returned and second party of like number took their place.	
do	11/4/16		Wet and cold. Unit arrangements. do	
do	12th to 14th		Training under unit arrangements	

INTELLIGENCE SUMMARY

(Erase heading not required.)

Summaries are contained in F. S. Regs., Part II. and the Staff Manual respectively. Title Pages will be prepared in manuscript.

Place	Date	Hour	Summary of Events and Information	Remarks and references to Appendices
BERGUETTE	15/4/16		Brigade left to take over position held by "C" Group 38th Division.	Appendix 2
LOISNES	16/4/16 to 17/4/16		179th Bde HQ become "C" Group HQ. Units in Group :- A/179. B/179. D/179. A/174. C/174. D/184. 1 Sec B/186. D/186. 1 Section B/179 - for counter battery work. Battery Positions :- A/179 ----- X.24.a.0.0. ½ B/179 ----- F.12.c.6.3. H.Q. X.28.a.7.8. ½ B/179 ----- F.5.c.9.1. (Counter battery) D/179 ----- X.30.c.y.1½ A/174 ----- X.22.d.8.4. C/174 ----- S.14.c.1.4. D/184 ----- F.4.d.4.8. ½ B/186 ----- X.24.c.2.6. D/186 ----- F.5.c.0.8.	
	18/4/16		Units carried out registration on three days, very few rounds fired. do	
	19/4/16		D/179 battery position shelled 11.30 to 12.50 p.m.	

INTELLIGENCE SUMMARY

(Erase heading not required.)

Summaries are contained in F.S. Regs., Part II. and the Staff Manual respectively. Title Pages will be prepared in manuscript.

Place	Date	Hour	Summary of Events and Information	Remarks and references to Appendices
LOISNES	20/4/16	8 AM	Work continued on Gun Pits, Telephonic communication. Some instructional shooting.	
	21/4/16	8 AM	do	
	22/4/16	8 AM	do	
	23/4/16	8 AM	Usual work on gun pits and normal amount of shooting.	
	24	8 AM	do	
	25/4	8 AM	Quiet day with good light for Observation. Several targets fired on mostly for instructional purposes. Hostile shelling normal.	
	26/4	8 AM	Quiet day as before.	
	27/4	8 AM	Slight amount of gas came over from AUCHY sector. Hostile and own shelling normal.	
	28/4	8 AM	Good light for Observation, work normal. Two reports of G.A.S. between 8 and 10, batteries opened fire falling fire 30 x eg. Gas did not however come this way and there was no attack in this sector.	
	29/4	8 AM	Quiet day. Good light for Observation.	
	30/4	8 AM	A very quiet day with little artillery activity on either side. Light hazy atmosphere.	

A M Kennard
Lieut-Col.
Cmdg 179th Bde. R.F.A.

APPENDIX.

39th DIVISIONAL ARTILLERY.

(Extract)

Operation Order No 3.

1. Personnel of the 39th Divisional Artillery will be attached to the 33rd Divisional Artillery for instruction as under:—

   119th Brigade. R.F.A.   2nd April 1916.

   A Battery   2 Officers   20 Other Ranks to B Battery 156th Brigade
   B   "   2   "   20   "   " C   "   162nd   "
   A   "   2   "   20   "   " D   "   168th   "

   Motor Busses will meet this personnel as under:—

   119th Brigade. R.F.A. — 3 Busses — Berguette — (O.16.c.8.9 Sheet 36 A) at 8.45 a.m. 2nd April 1916.

   ANNEQUIN (F 29 a 4.9 Sheet 36 B) by 2nd April by 39th Division — This party will be met at ANNEQUIN Artillery at 11.15 a.m. Guides furnished from 33rd Divisional Artillery at 11.15 a.m. Party will be returned up to and including 2nd April by 39th Division — after that date by units to which attached.

   Issued at 9 a.m. 31/3/16

   (Sd) G.C. DWYER
                Major
   BRIGADE MAJOR R.A.
   39th DIVISION ARTILLERY.

APPENDIX.

No. 2.

Secret.

39th Divisional Artillery.

Operation Order No. 4.

1. The 39th Division will relieve the 38th Division in the GIVENCHY and FESTUBERT sections of XI Corps Front.
2. 39th Div Arty relieves 38th Div Arty (and attached battery 33rd Div) on 14th and 15th April.
3. Batteries of 39th Div will relieve Batteries of 38th and 33rd Div as follows:—

Date.	Unit.	From. Wagon Lines	To Unit relieved	Unit relieved	Gun Position
April 14th	A/179 } 1 sec B/179 } each D/179	BERGUETTE " "	W.16.d.4.6 X.14.c.5.0 X.14.c.6.3	B/119 C/119 D/119	X.24.a.0.0. F.12.c.6.3. X.30.c.4.1½.
April 15th	HQ/179 A/179 } 1 sec B/179 } each D/179	" " " "	X.28.a.4.8 } as on 14th	"C" Group. H.Q. } as on 14th	} as on 14th
	C/179 BAC/179	19th DIV BERGUETTE	X.15.c.5.4. X.19.c.4.4.	BAC/119.	nil nil

39th Divisional Artillery.

179th BRIGADE

ROYAL FIELD ARTILLERY.

MAY 1916

179 RFA
Army Form C. 2118

XXXIX VOL. 3

WAR DIARY or INTELLIGENCE SUMMARY
(Erase heading not required.)

Instructions regarding War Diaries and Intelligence Summaries are contained in F. S. Regs., Part II. and the Staff Manual respectively. Title Pages will be prepared in manuscript.

Place	Date	Hour	Summary of Events and Information	Remarks and references to Appendices
LOISNES	1/5/16		Fairly quiet day, usual amount of hostile shelling, observation good but little hazy in morning.	
	2/5/16		Normal amount of activity, nothing unusual. Observation good.	
	3/5/16		Fairly quiet, work normal. Test S.O.S. during night, satisfactory.	
	4/5/16	9.50 P.M.	Wednesday, normal. G.A.S. alarm, fire opened 60 secs battery fire. Ceased firing 10:10.	
	4/5/16		Usual amount activity. Good light for observation.	
	5/5/16		Work normal, light good, slight rain in evening.	
	6/5/16		Work normal, light for observation good, slight showers at intervals.	
	7/5/16		Hostile shelling normal. "C" Battery went away for training under Col PRINGLE. Showers at intervals, light sufficient.	
			Work normal, light fair for observation.	
	8/5/16		Work normal, very little hostile shelling.	
	9/5/16		Weather bad, light very little use for observing consequently very little activity 25th on our front and enemy's. Work normal. Small amount	
	10/5/16		Light bad until 12 Noon then good. Work normal.	
	11/5/16		Light insufficient. Less activity than usual. Take gas alarm 9.50 P.M.	
	12/5/16		Light fair. Activity normal.	
	13/5/16		Rain all day, less activity than usual.	

Army Form C. 2118

WAR DIARY or INTELLIGENCE SUMMARY

(Erase heading not required.)

Instructions regarding War Diaries and Intelligence Summaries are contained in F.S. Regs., Part II. and the Staff Manual respectively. Title Pages will be prepared in manuscript.

Place	Date	Hour	Summary of Events and Information	Remarks and references to Appendices
LOISNES	14/5/16 to 15/5/16		Usual amount of activity with our own and hostile guns. Weather good.	
	16/5/16		Command of "C" Group taken over by Col. KILNER (Cmdg. 186th Bde. R.F.A.). Hdqrs. 179th Bde. removed to LOCON.	
	17/5/16			
	18/5/16 to 19/5/16		Q 36 a 9.3. Hdqrs. 179th Bde. in rest.	
	20/5/16		Composition of Bdes. reorganised. BAC absorbed into DAC and C/179 becomes C/186, B/186 becoming D/179 and D/179 becoming C/179, making 3 18/Pdr batteries and 1 4.5" How. battery in a Brigade.	
	24/5/16		Col. KENNARD became a/GOCRA during absence on tour of BRIG-GEN GILSON. Maj. HARLEY O.C. B/179 took command of 179th Bde. during the period Col. KENNARD away.	
LOCON	25/5/16 to 31/5/16		Hdqrs. in rest, batteries under control of Col. KILNER 186th Bde. R.F.A.	

A.M. Kennard
Lt. Col. Cmdg.
179 H.Bde. R.F.A.

39th Divisional Artillery.

179th BRIGADE

ROYAL FIELD ARTILLERY.

JUNE 1916

WAR DIARY or **INTELLIGENCE SUMMARY**
(Erase heading not required.)

Army Form C. 2118
179. R.F.A.
XXXIX
June Vol 3
1916

June 1916

Place	Date	Hour	Summary of Events and Information	Remarks and references to Appendices
LOCON	1/5/16 to 11/5/16		Headquarters still in rest billets.	
	12/5/16		One section D battery relieved one section D/121 Bde and came into orders of 61st Divl Artillery at L.36.C.5.4. (Maroc Sheet 36a BETHUNE)	
	13/5/16		Remaining section of D completed the relief.	
	14/6/16		Nothing to report. 16/6/16. Col Kennard resumed command of Bde.	
	15/-/-		One section D battery returned to 39 H Bn Arty and went into action at F.5.C.5.6.	
	16/-/-			
	17/-/-			
	18/-/-		Remaining section D returned as above section	
	19/-/-		Bde Hdqrs removed to W.6.d.5.2.	
	20/-/-		Everything normal. 'C' Bty	
	27/-/-		2/Lieut F.M. STROUVELLE wounded by shrapnel. Capt MADELEY comdg 'C' Battery sick, command taken over by 2/Lieut W.S. DURWARD, Adjutant.	
	28/-/-			
	29/-/- to 30/-/-		Normal.	

AM Kennard
Lt. Col. Commanding
Commanding 179th Brigade, R.F.A.

39th Divisional Artillery.

179th BRIGADE

ROYAL FIELD ARTILLERY.

JULY 1916

HQ 39th R.A.

Herewith "WAR DIARY" Volume I for month of July 1916.

31/7/16

CM Longley Lt
Adjutant
for O.C. 179th Bde. R.F.A.

July Army Form C. 2118
179 R.F.A.
Vol 5

WAR DIARY
or
INTELLIGENCE SUMMARY
(Erase heading not required.)

Instructions regarding War Diaries and Intelligence Summaries are contained in F.S. Regs., Part II. and the Staff Manual respectively. Title Pages will be prepared in manuscript.

Place	Date	Hour	Summary of Events and Information	Remarks and references to Appendices
LOCON	1/7/16	0th	Battery positions at beginning of month. Reference map 1:40.000 combined sheet BETHUNE.	
			Unit. Gun Position. Wagon Line.	
			Headquarters W.6.d.5.2 (in rest)	
			A Battery X.24.a.0.0. X.25.Central.	
			B " F.12.c.6.3. (2 guns)	
			F.6.a.0.5. (2 guns) X.19.c.4.7.	
			C " X.30.C.7.1½ X.14.c.6.0.	
			D " F.5.c.5.6. X.25.d.1.0.	
			A, B and C batteries in "C" Group 39th Divisional Artillery Commanded by Col. KILNER (O.C. 186th Bde. R.F.A.).	
			D. Battery attached to 33rd Divisional Artillery.	
2nd		0th	Programmes as laid down by 39th R.A. H.Qrs carried out by all batteries.	
3rd		0th	Batteries in "C" Group cooperated in raid on German trenches, bombardment starting 11.30 P.M and continuing on until next morning.	
4th		0th	Nothing to report	
5th		0th		
6th		0th		

WAR DIARY or INTELLIGENCE SUMMARY

Army Form C. 2118

Place	Date	Hour	Summary of Events and Information	Remarks and references to Appendices
TOURBIERES	7/7/16		Headquarters left LOCON and went to TOURBIERES (F.23.d.9.7). Col KENNARD took over command of Cuinchy Group. (Extract from Operation Order No.19 issued by 39th R.A. dated July 6th 1916. C/179 relieves C/167 at F.24.a.3.8. ½ B/179 " ½ C/166 " A.14.c.9.7. HQ/179th Bde will assume responsibility for CUINCHY GROUP at 4.0 P.M. tomorrow.) CUINCHY GROUP made up as follows. C/184 at F.24.C.6.8. C/179 " F.24.a.3.8. A/184 " F.24.a.2/2.3/2. A/186 " F.30.a.9.7. ½ B/179 " A.14.C.9.7. D/174 " A.20.C.4.7. D/184 " F.30.C.1.4. The Zone supported by this Group extends from A.22.a.1.8 in the North to G.4.a.8.8 in the South.	Ref Map BETHUNE 1/40,000 Combined sheet.

WAR DIARY or INTELLIGENCE SUMMARY

Army Form C. 2118

Place	Date	Hour	Summary of Events and Information	Remarks and references to Appendices
TOURBIERES	7/7/16	9ᵗʰ	Extreme limit of zone able to be covered by guns in the group extends from A16 a 5.5 (where enemy's front line crosses the LA BASSÉE CANAL) to H19 a 7.5 (South of HULLUCH)	
	8/7/16	9ᵗʰ	At 12 Midnight on night of 7/8ᵗʰ Infantry strong & small mines at different points on this front. 1 at MAD POINT (A28 c B2) 1 just North of the LA BASSÉE ROAD and two at JENNOWEEN HILL. A Barrage was placed behind all mines by the artillery, fire opening at 12. Midnight and pausing from 12.5 to 12.15 AM when firing continued to 12.20 when it ceased altogether and the front became normal again. Fairly quiet day.	
		10ᵗʰ	Normal activity during daylight. At 11.30 P.M. Artillery 3 batteries D/184, A/186, and C/184 assisted in a raid carried out by the Group on right, firing ceased at 12.10 AM. after our own Infantry had withdrawn. (Result successful) Normal.	
		11ᵗʰ		
		12ᵗʰ		
		13ᵗʰ	Retaliation on enemy's Minenwerfer at 10.0 a.m. and again at 9.30 P.M.	
		14ᵗʰ	Extract from 39ᵗʰ Div Operation order No 22 dated 14/7/16	

WAR DIARY
or
INTELLIGENCE SUMMARY
(Erase heading not required.)

Army Form C. 2118

Place	Date	Hour	Summary of Events and Information	Remarks and references to Appendices
TOURBIERES			1. The following moves will take place tonight:— 1 Section C/179 to F.11.b.4.4. and comes under orders of O.C. B/186 1 " B/179 " F.10.d.7.6. " " " " " C/186 1 " A/186 " X.24.c.6.9 " " " " " C/186 1 " C/184 " F.4.d.4.8 " " " " " B/184 2. Sections of the batteries at present forming Cuinchy Group will be relieved tonight and tomorrow night by sections of 15" R.A who will bring guns to wagon lines about midnight - (4 more) arriving at gun positions this afternoon. 3. Remaining sections of CUINCHY Group not mentioned in Para 1 will be ready to move tonight and orders as to their destinations will be issued later. 6. HQ 179 H Bde will be in readiness to move on completion of relief of batteries. 7. B/179 belonging to FESTUBERT Group will also be in readiness to move tonight if required.	

LACOUTURE 15th			Left CUINCHY. Arrived FERME DU BOIS Group. (F.F. GROUP)
			 Group composed of following units. HQrs at X.4.b.6.8.
			
			 31st DW { A/165 4.18/hr at S.7.b.3.9.
			            { B/165 4.18/hr " M.26.a.3.0.
			
			            { D/174 4. 4.5 How " M.32.6.4.3.
			 1st { A/184 4.18/hr " M.32.c.9.7.
			 39th DW { C/184 2. " " S.7.d.7½.6.
			            { D/184 4.4.5 How " X.17.d.9½.9½.
			            A/186 2.18/hr " S.1.d.4.8.	

WAR DIARY or INTELLIGENCE SUMMARY

(Erase heading not required.)

Army Form C. 2118

Place	Date	Hour	Summary of Events and Information	Remarks and references to Appendices
LACOUTURE	16th 17th 18th		Registration and work on gun pits etc.	
	19th 20th		Breaches made in enemy's parapet.	
	21st		Support given to Infantry during company operations.	Appm 1
	22		Operation as per O.O. 3.	
	23		Quiet day.	2
	24		See Appendix 2	
	25		Quiet day.	
	26		Left FERME DU BOIS group and took over FESTUBERT Group. A battery went into rest billets. Registration by new Batteries.	
LOISNES	27th 28		Observation & Registration. Wire cutting and fixation against parapets. Usual work.	3
	29			
	30	night	Operations as per O.O. 12	
	31	day	More than usual activity by enemy's heavies on front line.	
	31		2/Lieut O.A: GAMM evacuated sick to England during month.	

Army Form C. 2118

WAR DIARY
or
INTELLIGENCE SUMMARY
(Erase heading not required.)

Place	Date	Hour	Summary of Events and Information	Remarks and references to Appendices
LOISNES			2/Lieut. R. GOUGH posted to A Battery. 2/Lieut. C.S. HODGKINSON " C " " 2/Lieut. C.G. GAME. " HQ as Orderly Officer 2/Lieut. F.H. STROUVELLE evacuated to Base Guard (wounded). CAPTAIN D.J. MADRLET " " (sick). LIEUT. W.S. DURWARD posted to Command C Battery. 2/Lieut. C.W. LONGLEY appointed Adjutant.	

AMKennard
Lt. Col.
Officer Comdg 179th Bde. R.F.A.

SECRET.

Copy No 10

Of

OPERATION ORDER No 3.

UNIT	TIME	TARGET	REMARKS
A/165 A/174 A/180 B/165 C/184 D/174 D/184	3.20 P.M.	S.11.c.1½.9¾	4 Rounds Per Gun - Endeavour to breach the parapet

To take place during day of 22nd instant
Acknowledge by 'Phone.
Issued at 10.0 am. 22.7.16.

Copy No 1 to A/165
    2 to A/184
    3 to A/180
    4 to B/165
    5 to C/184
    6 to D/174
    7 to D/184
    8 to Infantry
    9 to File

Arthur R.R.M.?
Adjutant F. Group.

SECRET.
ZERO TIME 11 P.M.

"F" Gough OPERATION ORDER No 5.   Copy No. 14

Operation to take trenches on night of 23rd/24th July 1916

BATTERY	No OF GUNS	TIME FROM H.M.	TIME TO H.M.	TARGET	No OF ROUNDS	REMARKS
D/174	2	0.10	0.32	S.11.a.8.8½ to S.11.a.7¾.5	22	METHOD OF FIRE left to discretion of B.C.'s. so long as 2 round per ½
	1	0.12	0.32	S.11.c.5.3½	10	
	1	0.12	0.32	S.11.a.1.1.	10	
D/184	2	0.12	0.32	S.10.d.8.2¾	20	How. bee. minute
	2	0.12	0.32	MACHINE GUNS AT S.10.d.5.5	20	Trench bet.turnpermin are fired
B/165	3	0.12	0.32	COMMUNICATION TRENCH FROM S.10.d.6.6. TO S.10.d.8.2¼.	120	18 pdrs to fire H.E. only
A/186	3	0.12	0.32	S.10.d.6.6 To S.10.d.8.2¾	120	
C/184	2	0.12	0.32	S.10.d.8.2¼ To S.11.c.5.3½	80	
A/165	3	0.12	0.32	S.10.d.8.2¾ To S.11.c.5.3½	120	
A/184	3	0.12	0.32	S.11.c.5.3½ To S.11.c.1.9½	120	
C/174	4	0.12	0.32	S.10.d.8.2¼ To S.11.c.5.3½	160	
				TOTAL	802	

ACKNOWLEDGE. — Issued at 9pm 22nd July 1916

COPIES TO 1 – D/174   7 – A/184
2 – D/184   8 – C/174
3 – B/165   9 – 116th Infantry Bde. H.Q
4 – A/186   10 – FILE
5 – C/184   11 – H.Q. 39TH DIV. ARTY
6 – A/165   12-13 – WAR DIARY.

"F" Gough.
Lt Commanding

SECRET.   "C" GROUP. R.F.A.   Copy No. 16

OPERATION ORDER No. 12 (This cancels Operation Order No. 11)

To take place on night of 30/31 July. Zero time to be notified later.

UNIT	Nos. Guns	TARGET	FROM TIME	TO	REMARKS
C 186	4	Front parapet from A.3.d.6.4. to A.3.d.4.8	0.0.	0.5.	Shrapnel 3 rounds per gun per minute.
A 186	4	As above			
A 186	2	A.3.d.6.2.			
A 186	4	Mackensen's Support Trench from A.4.C.1/2.3/2. to A.3.b.8.3/4.2.			
C 186	4	C186 North Half } Division at A.3.d.9.8. A186 South Half } A.E.d.9.8.	0.5	Until Ordered to stop by "C" Group. H.Q.	3 rounds per 18 pdr. per minute and 1½ rounds per 4.5 Howitzer per minute.
A 184	4	Communication Trench from A.3.b.3.1. to A.3.b.8.3/4.2.			
D 186	1	A.4.C.1/2. 3/2.			H.E. only.
	1	A.3.d.6.2.			
	1	A.3.b.8.3/4.2.			
	1	A.3.b.3.1.			
D 184	4	Papier Mose.			
"B" Group 2-18 pdr 2-How		A.9.b.2.4. to A.9.b.7.6.	0.0.	Until ordered to stop by "C" Group H.Q.	
C 184	4	Front parapet from S.22.C.5.3/4.7. to S.22.C.9.3/4.3 { Minus 10 }		0.10/15	
Right Group 2-18 pdr 2-4.5 How 51st Div		Support Trench from S.22.C.6.8. to S.22.d.1/2.3 3/4.			

Acknowledge.   Issued at 7.0.p.m. 29/7/16.

(W.) Wrigley
Adjutant C Group
For O.C. C. Group.

39th Divisional Artillery.

179th BRIGADE

ROYAL FIELD ARTILLERY.

AUGUST 1 9 1 6 ::::

WAR DIARY or INTELLIGENCE SUMMARY

Army Form C. 2118

149th Brigade RFA
Vol 6
From 1st to 31st August 1916

Place	Date	Hour	Summary of Events and Information	Remarks and references to Appendices
LOISNES	1/8/16		Brigade in action in Givenchy sector all except A battery who were in rest.	
	2/8/16		D battery relieved at F.5.c.5.6 by D/174.	
			A — went into action at A.7.d.7½.3 relieving B/174	
	3/8/16			
	5/8/16		Nothing unusual to report.	
	6/8/16		From 10 a.m. to 2 p.m. B battery were shelled with 5.9 about 200 one man only wounded, no guns damaged.	
	7/8		Usual activity on this front, nothing unusual.	
	7/8/16		2/Lieut. C. SIMPSON killed by 77 mm shell while attending to the wires at forward gun position of C/186 in INDIAN VILLAGE.	
	8/to 10/-		Usual work and activity.	
LIERES	11/8/16		Withdrawn from the line and marched to LIERES.	
ROELLECOURT	12/		Left LIERES 7.45 p.m. and marched to MONCHEY-BRETON training area. Brigade bivouced around ROELLECOURT.	
	13 to 20		Training	
	21 &			
	15th		Col KENNARD evacuated sick. Major HARLEY took command of Brigade.	

WAR DIARY or INTELLIGENCE SUMMARY

Army Form C. 2118

Place	Date	Hour	Summary of Events and Information	Remarks and references to Appendices
POELLCOURT	19/8/16		Col. A. EARDLEY-WILMOT took over command of the Brigade. 2nd Lieut. PRATT posted to C Battery on promotion.	
	20th			
LUCHEUX	21st		Left POELLCOURT and marched to LUCHEUX about 15 miles.	
THIEVRES	22nd		Left LUCHEUX and marched to THIEVRES about 6 miles.	
	23 & 24		Bde remained at THIEVRES	
	25th		Batteries marched to Wagon Lines at BERTRAN COURT.	
	25th		Hdqrs marched to billets at BUS-LES-ARTOIS.	
BUS-LES-ARTOIS.	26th		Batteries took guns into action at following places:— Ref Map Sheet 57d. S.E. 1:20,000.	
	26		A) batteries Q.13.d.8.6 to Q.14.a.3.5 under command of B) Colonel Allardyce (174th Bde RFA) C battery being attached 1/2 to A and 1/2 to B making three batteries 6 gun batteries, A being commanded by Capt. BELL and B by Maj. HARLEY. D battery at Q.20.a.2.1 under Colonel ALLARDYCE.	
	27th		Weather showery. Batteries worked on new positions.	
	28th		do. Batteries carried out registration and took part in bombardment during the afternoon.	
	29			

WAR DIARY
or
INTELLIGENCE SUMMARY

Army Form C. 2118

Place	Date	Hour	Summary of Events and Information	Remarks and references to Appendices
BUS. LES - ARTOIS	30/12		Weather very bad. Operations postponed 24 hours.	
	31/12		Weather better. 2/Lieut. FORTUNE joined Brigade. Major H.K. HARLEY struck off strength of Brigade on Medical grounds in England.	

R. Earley Wilmot
Col.
Officer Commanding
179th Brigade. R.F.A.

War Diary

179th Bde
R.F.A.

Volume 1

Month of August 1916

39th Divisional Artillery.

179th BRIGADE

ROYAL FIELD ARTILLERY

SEPTEMBER 1 9 1 6:

WAR DIARY
or
INTELLIGENCE SUMMARY
(Erase heading not required.)

Army Form C. 2118

Period 1st to 30th Sept 1916

179. R.F.A. Vol I Vol 7

30 Div

Place	Date	Hour	Summary of Events and Information	Remarks and references to Appendices
BUS-LES-ARTOIS.	1/9/1916		Batteries in action at following points. Ref Map. Sheet 57 D 1:40,000.	
			A. Batt. Q.14.c.08.15.	
			B. " Q.14.a.09.16.	
			C. " 1 section attached to A and one to B.	
			D. " Q.20.a.27.00.	
			Hdqrs at BUS-LES-ARTOIS.	
	2nd		Preliminary bombardment for attack on 3rd.	
	3rd		Batteries supported attack by 39th Div. Infantry.	
	4th		Usual activity.	
	5th		Batteries moved to following positions:-	
			A Batt K.32.d.2.3 relieved C Batt 39th Bde.	
			B " Q.1.b.8.3 " B " "	
			C " Q.2.a.1.9 " A " "	
			D " K.32.c.57.53. " D " "	
			Hdqrs moved to MAILLY-MAILLET at Q.7.C.8.8. to take charge of W. Group consisting of the batteries of 179th Bde only relieving left Group of 11th Division. Infantry supported two battalions of 145 + 148 Bde 48th Div.	
MAILLY MAILLET			Batteries registered in new positions.	
	6th		At 2.30 a.m. Infantry at left Battalion asked for retaliation on hostile trench mortars. MAILLY-MAILLET shelled from 12.30 to 3.30 a.m.	
	7th			

WAR DIARY
or
INTELLIGENCE SUMMARY

(Erase heading not required.)

Army Form C. 2118

Place	Date	Hour	Summary of Events and Information	Remarks and references to Appendices
MAILLY-MAILLET.	8th		Registration by batteries.	
	9th		do. do.	
	10th	3.0 to 3.10 p.m.	Barrage on enemy's support line carried out by all batteries, 20 rounds per gun expended.	
	11th	Night of 10th.	145th Inf Bde relieved by 116th Inf Bde. 39th Div.	
	12th		Wire-cutting and registration of "Tudor Hole". Registration of Concentration Lines. 6 minute bombardment of enemy reserve trench.	
	13th		Usual work. Enemy trench mortars shelled and silenced by 'D' Battery.	
	14th		Usual work. Enemy trench mortars active in early morning.	
	15th		Inter-Battalion reliefs on this sector.	
	16th		Usual work. Several requests by infantry for retaliation on enemy trench mortars.	
	17th		Evening HQ shelled at MAILLY-MAILLET and have set on fire.	
	18th		Allowance of ammunition cut down to 60 rounds per 18 pdr battery and 40 rounds per Howitzer battery per day.	
	19th		Frequent requests for retaliation on hostile trench mortars very active. 116th Infantry Bde extended their front, taking over from 2nd Division.	
	20th		Usual work by batteries, hostile trench mortars again active. Retaliation with 18 pdr how and 18 pdr on enemy front line, shelling ceased.	

Army Form C. 2118

WAR DIARY
or
INTELLIGENCE SUMMARY
(Erase heading not required.)

Instructions regarding War Diaries and Intelligence Summaries are contained in F.S. Regs., Part II. and the Staff Manual respectively. Title Pages will be prepared in manuscript.

Place	Date	Hour	Summary of Events and Information	Remarks and references to Appendices
MAILLY MAILLET.	20-9-16		Headquarters moved from MAILLY-MAILLET to a camp in the area at P.6.a.2.3. The composition of the Group being altered owing to 39th Div taking over the whole Vth Corps front. The following batteries composed group :—	
			A 179 39th Div at K.32.d.2.3. 4 guns	
			B 179 do " Q.1.b.8.3. 4 guns	
			D 179 do " K.32.c.6.3. 4 hows	
			50th Bty 2nd Div " Q.2.c.4.3. 6 guns	
			70th Bty do " K.31.c.7.3 and K.31.c.8/2.6/2. 6 guns	
			58th Bty do " Q.1.d.3/2.7. 4 hows	
			X 39 M.T.M. Bty { 2 Guns in BROADWAY.	
			2 " " HOUNSLOW STREET.	
			X 2 M.T.M. Bty 2 " " K.34.b.4.4.	
			2 " " K.34.d.7.3.	
			Infantry supported 116th Infantry Brigade with all Battalions in the line. Group now called 'Centre' Group with Right Group 39th Div and Left Group 39th Div Arty on Right and Left respectively.	

WAR DIARY
or
INTELLIGENCE SUMMARY
(Erase heading not required.)

Army Form C. 2118

Place	Date	Hour	Summary of Events and Information	Remarks and references to Appendices
P.6.a.k.3.	21.9.16		C/179 having been withdrawn from Centre Group and placed in Left Group. Zones allotted to A & B batteries altered to cover new front. Registration carried out on new Zones. Several requests for retaliation during day and night - all of which received attention, fairly quiet day on the whole.	
	22.9.16		Quiet day.	
BEAUSART	23.9.16		Left P.6.a.k.3 and removed H.Q. to BEAUSART (Billet No. 36).	
	24 } 25 }		Organised Bombardment of hostile front and support line system by all batteries in the group, special amount of ammunition being allowed for the purpose. Retaliation by enemy for this bombardment weak.	A
	26th	12.35	Feint attack on this front. Artillery programme shewn in Appendix A. Retaliation by enemy with 5.9 and x.x resulted in all M.T.M guns being knocked out	
	27th		Enemy batteries engaged by counter-batteries. Repairs to T.M. emplacements.	
	28th		Counter-battery work, several batteries engaged which the enemy were suspected of moving.	
	29th		Very quiet day. Weather bad.	
	30th		Wire-cutting by 18 pdrs. Howitzers on enemy O.Ps. 116th By/ 13.de relieved by 99th Bde from M.34.B.9.0.25 M.35.a.35.90 (1 Battalion)	

C. Earnley-Wilmot
Lt Col
Officer Commanding 179th Bde RFA

SECRET

GROUP OPERATION ORDER No. 2.
Reference R.A/43/1/G dated 23.9.16.

FEINT ATTACK

The part allotted to CENTRE GROUP is sub-divided as follows:—

PHASE	UNIT	TARGET
I	70th Battery	K.35.a.9.2 to K.35.d.½.5½
	A/179	K.35.d.½.5½ to K.35.d.1.0
	50th Battery	K.35.d.1.0 to Q.5.c.2.5.
II	70th Battery	K.35.a.2.2½ to K.35.c.2½.2½
	A/179	K.35.c.2½.2½ to Q.5.a.2.7½
	50th Battery	Q.5.a.2.7½ to Q.5.c.2.8½
	B/179	Q.5.c.2.8½ to Q.4.d.9.5
III	AS IN PHASE I	
IV	AS IN PHASE II	
V	Each Battery fire on Support Line as in Phase I and also enfilade C.T's leading up to it.	

SHEET. 2

In addition to Batteries specially selected in the Order the following Batteries will be prepared to concentrate if called upon.

UNIT	TASKS
A/179	H as shown J.K.L.M
B/179	H.J.K.L.M.
50th Battery	J.K.L.M.
56th Battery	J. as shown.

BATTERY COMMANDERS PLEASE NOTE TASK.. N.

SECRET

GROUP OPERATION ORDER No. 2.
REFERENCE R.A/43/1/G DATED 23.9.16.

FEINT ATTACK

The part allotted to CENTRE GROUP is sub-divided as follows:-

PHASE	UNIT	TARGET
I	70TH BATTERY	K.35.a.9.2 To K.35.d.$\frac{1}{2}$.5$\frac{1}{2}$
	A/179	K.35.d.$\frac{1}{2}$.5$\frac{1}{2}$ To K.35.d.1.0
	50TH BATTERY	K.35.d.1.0 To Q.5.c.2.5
II	70TH BATTERY	K.35.a.2.2$\frac{1}{2}$ To K.35.c.2$\frac{1}{2}$.2$\frac{1}{2}$
	A/179	K.35.c.2$\frac{1}{2}$.2$\frac{1}{2}$ To Q.5.a.2.7$\frac{1}{2}$
	50TH BATTERY	Q.5.a.2.7$\frac{1}{2}$ To Q.5.c.2.8$\frac{1}{2}$
	B/179	Q.5.c.2.8$\frac{1}{2}$ To Q.4.d.9.5
III	AS IN PHASE. I	
IV	AS IN PHASE. II	
V	EACH BATTERY FIRE ON SUPPORT LINE AS IN PHASE. I AND ALSO ENFILADE C.T's LEADING UP TO IT.	

SHEET. 2

In addition to Batteries specially selected in the Order, the following Batteries will be prepared to concentrate if called upon.

UNIT	TASKS
A/179	H as shown J.K.L.M
B/179	H.J.K.L.M.
50TH BATTERY	J.K.L.M.
56TH BATTERY	J. as shown.

BATTERY COMMANDERS PLEASE NOTE TASK.. N.

39th Divisional Artillery.

179th BRIGADE

ROYAL FIELD ARTILLERY

OCTOBER 1 9 1 6:

Vol 8

WAR DIARY
INTELLIGENCE SUMMARY

179th Brigade R.F.A.
Vol. I. No. 8 Period 1st - 31st October 1916

Army Form C. 2118

Place	Date	Hour	Summary of Events and Information	Remarks and references to Appendices
BEAUSART	1/10/16		Group same as at end of last month. Quiet day.	
	2/10/16		50th and 70th Batteries left the group and went back to 2nd Div. C/179 relieved 50th and C/186 came into group at Q.2.c.4.3.	
VITERMONT	3/10/16		Bde HQ left BEAUSSART and went to VITERMONT. 39th Division left Vth Corps and came into IInd Corps. Group now consisted of the following. Ref Sheet 57d 1:40,000.	

Group HQ at ———— Q.13.d.6.8.
A/179 ———— K.32.d.3.2.
B/179 ———— Q.1.b.8.3.
C/179 ———— Q.2.a.1½.9.
D/179 ———— K.32.b.5½.
C/186 ———— Q.2.c.4.3.
C/174 ———— Q.13.d.9.6.
56th Bde (2nd R.A.) ———— Q.1.d.4.7.

Front covered from WATLING STREET (Q.4.6.5½.6.) to CARLISLE ST. (Q.10.d.5½.4.) held by 116th Infantry Bde with two battalions in the line.

Army Form C. 2118

WAR DIARY
or
INTELLIGENCE SUMMARY
(Erase heading not required.)

Place	Date	Hour	Summary of Events and Information	Remarks and references to Appendices
VITERMONT	3/10/16		Wagon Lines moved from LOUVENCOURT to field S.W. of HEDAUVILLE. During the day several requests received from Infantry for retaliation for enemy trench mortars and rifle grenades. During the night at odd intervals C/179 and B/179 shelled enemy communication trenches and roads leading up to their front in all 120 rounds being fired. Right Group was Right Group 39th Division. Group on our left was Right Group 2nd Division, group on right Right Group 39th Division. Intermittent shelling of enemy front and support lines at odd intervals during night.	
	5/10/16		Quiet day. Programme similar to that of 4th during night.	
	6/10/16		Weather good. do do	
	7/10/16		Night bombardment of enemy trench system.	
	8/10/16		Wire cut at Q.5.a.2.3 and Q.10.b.7.1/2. Night shelling of enemy trenches as before.	
	9/10/16		From 10–12.30 p.m and again from 1.0 to 4.30 p.m. enemy front and support trenches bombarded. Night programme as before. Gaps started in 8th enlarged.	

WAR DIARY
or
INTELLIGENCE SUMMARY

(Erase heading not required.)

Army Form C. 2118

Place	Date	Hour	Summary of Events and Information	Remarks and references to Appendices
VITERMONT	12/10/16 to 13/10/16		Usual activity. Night firing by all batteries on enemy's front-line, support line and communication trenches.	
	14th		Attack on SCHWABEN REDOUBT by 118th Inf Bde. Batteries assisted in barrage. Attack successful. C/175 withdrawn from group.	
	15th		Gas shell fired on BEAUMONT HAMEL by D/179.	
	16th	9.30 to 10.30 P.M.	Continuous shelling of enemy trench system.	
	17th		Usual activity. Relief of batteries by batteries of 51st Division by sections.	
ENGLEBELMER	18th		Battery relief completed. HQ taken over by Col DUNCAN 255th Bde RFA.	
	19th		This Brigade moved to south of ENGLEBELMER. Batteries also moved further south. Registration of new front.	

WAR DIARY
or
INTELLIGENCE SUMMARY

(Erase heading not required.)

Army Form C. 2118

Place	Date	Hour	Summary of Events and Information	Remarks and references to Appendices
ENGLEBELMER	20/10/16		New front from Q11c54 to Q17a 9.7. registered.	
	21/10/16		3 Batteries of 184 1st Bde came under the control of this Bde and new group called No 1 Group formed, the whole under the orders of 51st Div. Batteries in group. A.B.C. D/179. A.B. D/184. 253rd Bde on the left and A group consisting of 39th Div 253rd Bde on the left and A group consisting of 39th Div batteries under Col ALLARDYCE (174 Bde). A Group under control of 63rd DIV.	
	22/10/16		Registration by all batteries.	
	23/10/16		Barrage scheme for 51st Division worked out - a registered. Wire cutting along front. Registration for 63rd Div Barrage. Night firing. Night firing on enemy's C.T. and reserve lines.	
	24 to 28		Wire cutting. Weather wet and windy.	
	29th		As before, weather bad.	

WAR DIARY or INTELLIGENCE SUMMARY

Army Form C. 2118

Place	Date	Hour	Summary of Events and Information	Remarks and references to Appendices
ENGLEBELMER	30/10/16		Weather still very bad. Unable to cut wire. Night firing as usual.	
	31/10/16		Weather better. Wire cutting. Night firing.	

A. Emden-Stuart.
Colonel.
Officer Commanding
179th Bde. R.F.A.

39th Divisional Artillery.

179th BRIGADE

ROYAL FIELD ARTILLERY.

NOVEMBER 1 9 1 6

Army Form C. 2118

WAR DIARY
or
INTELLIGENCE SUMMARY
(Erase heading not required.)

179 Brigade RFA

Place	Date	Hour	Summary of Events and Information	Remarks and references to Appendices
ENGLEBELMER	12th 11/16		Group as at end of last month. Daily and nightly bombardment of enemy trenches. Wire cutting when weather favourable. Weather mostly wet and misty.	
	13/11/16		Attack on BEAUMONT HAMEL commenced 5.45 A.M. all batteries in group assisted in barrage for 51st Div., firing all day until objective beyond village taken. Night firing kept up all night beyond line held by Infantry.	
	14/11/16		Advance continued at 5.50 AM to Munich Trench.	
	15/11/16		Protective fire beyond infantry who were consolidating Munich Trench.	
	16/11/16		Group ceased to be under 51st D.A. and came under orders of 63rd D.A.	
	17/11/16		Casualties during attack. Officer CPT DURRANT B/184 killed, 1 man A/179 wounded. On 14th and 2 men of A/184 killed, 1 man A/179 wounded. Weather cold and frosty but fine. No firing.	

WAR DIARY or INTELLIGENCE SUMMARY

Army Form C. 2118

(Erase heading not required.)

Instructions regarding War Diaries and Intelligence Summaries are contained in F. S. Regs., Part II. and the Staff Manual respectively. Title Pages will be prepared in manuscript.

Place	Date	Hour	Summary of Events and Information	Remarks and references to Appendices
	18/11/16		Unsuccessful Batteries much strained. Now registration.	
	19/11/16		Barrage for 18th Div attack on FRANKFURT TRENCH. Came out of action, batteries went to wagon lines, HQ to BOUZINCOURT.	
	20/11/16		March to 2nd Army commenced went to AMPLIER to billets.	
	21/11/16		Continued march and billeted at MONCHEL.	
	22/11/16		March continued to HESTRUS.	
	23 & 24th		} Rested at HESTRUS.	
	25th		March continued to RELY.	
	26th		do to STEENBECQUE.	
	27th		do to ARNEKE.	
ARNEKE	28th		Reorganization of D.A. commenced. C/179 divided Right section to A battery and Left section to B battery making A & B batteries 6-gun batteries.	
	29th		D/184 joined the Brigade and became C/179.	

WAR DIARY
or
INTELLIGENCE SUMMARY

(Erase heading not required.)

Place	Date	Hour	Summary of Events and Information	Remarks and references to Appendices
ARNEKE	30/11/16		Reorganization of Bde complete at midnight. Bde now composed as under:-	
			A battery 6-gun 18 pdr (Old A/179 and Right Section Old C/179)	
			B — 6 — 18 — (Old B/179 and Left Section Old C/179)	
			C — 4-gun 4.5 How (Old D/184)	
			D — 4 — 4.5 — (As before).	

A. Ennthy Wilmot
Lt Col
Officer Cmdg 179th Bde RFA.

39th Divisional Artillery.

179th BRIGADE

ROYAL FIELD ARTILLERY.

DECEMBER 1 9 1 6

WAR DIARY
or
INTELLIGENCE SUMMARY

(Erase heading not required.)

Army Form C. 2118

179 Bde R.F.A. Vol 6

Place	Date	Hour	Summary of Events and Information	Remarks and references to Appendices
ARNEKE	1/12/16		Brigade resting at ARNEKE.	
	6/12/16			
WATOU	7/12/16		Whole Brigade less C battery moved to WATOU. Advance party proceeded direct to ELVERDINGHE to take over telephone communications.	
	8/12/16		Section of each A B and D moved up into action.	
ELVERDINGHE	9/12/16		Other section came up into action and HQ took over from BELGIAN ARTY.	
			Battery Positions :-	
			HQ. B 8 d 8 7	
			Ref. Sheet 28 NW A. Batt. 4 guns B 8 d 5250	
			1:20000 2 guns T 21 a 8 2 and T 21 d 4 8	
			Sheet 20 SW B. Batt. 6 guns B 8 b 7.0.16 B 8 b 75.27. ~~B.14.b.4.8/4.~~	
			1:20000 D. Batt. 2 How's	
	10/12/16		Registration. C battery came up into action at 1.2.c.8.3.	
	/16		1st section do do do	
	14/12/16		(Other Section of C do do C.25.d.5.2½.	
	15/12/16		Other Section of D do do do	
	16/12/16		Bde D.A. visited in action by Army Commander (2nd Army).	
	17/12/16		Poor visibility owing to sudden fogs. Battery positions cleared of much refuse left by previous	
	18/12/16		occupants, and drainage carried out.	
	19/12/16		Retaliated 54 Rds on German support line, BABY LANE, STEAM MILL for hostile minenwerfer.	

WAR DIARY
or
INTELLIGENCE SUMMARY

Army Form C. 2118

Place	Date	Hour	Summary of Events and Information	Remarks and references to Appendices
ELVERDINGHE (cont)	20/12/16		Fine & cold. Some aerial activity. Retaliated on German support line for hostile minenwerfer.	
	21/12/16 22/12/16		Slight hostile artillery activity during morning. Enfilade section registered on enemy front line. Wind & rain, becoming a gale at times. Again retaliated at infantry's request, for hostile minenwerfer & heavy shelling about 4pm.	
	23/12/16	2.45 am	Retaliated on enemy support lines for heavy hostile minenwerfer activity. Fired 48 rds. Heavy Artillery Group also fired some 6" hows. & the enemy were silenced after causing our infantry much annoyance.	Graves afterwards ascertained that the enemy had raided our Trenches.
		2 pm 3.15 pm	Carried out a reprisal bombardment on enemy front line (our front line being temporarily evacuated by the infantry). Satisfactory shoot, but owing to a gale following, probably most of the rounds were slightly blown.	
	24/12/16		Fine & sunny early, becoming overcast later. Working party dispersed. Registration of defence lines carried out. One target registered by aeroplane observation. Effective retaliation for hostile minenwerfer in evening.	
	25/12/16		Slow, continuous bombardment of enemy support lines, one round per hour on enemy hundred yards of the front, with the object of preventing fraternizing, from 7.30 am to 4.30 pm. Enemy replied at 4-4.30 pm with heavy minnies on our support line, which were silenced by our retaliatory fire. An S.O.S. call was received shortly before 10pm & batteries immediately opened fire. The S.O.S. was cancelled shortly afterwards.	

WAR DIARY or INTELLIGENCE SUMMARY

Army Form C. 2118

Place	Date	Hour	Summary of Events and Information	Remarks and references to Appendices
ELVERDINGHE	26/12/16		Fine & sunny early, becoming misty about 2 p.m. At 1.5 p.m. retaliation was requested for hostile minenwerfer on Centre Coy's front. Batteries opened fire within 2 minutes and effectively silenced the enemy, but another minenwerfer opened fire at 4.30 pm, which in turn was shelled by our howitzers and silenced.	
	27/12/16		Very fine & frosty. Visibility good between 10 and 3.30 pm. A battery was engaged and registered by our howitzer section at V.25.a.1.5.0, observed by Kite Balloon Section. Several barrage points registered by 18pdr batteries.	
	28/12/16		Visibility very poor all day. At 4.9 pm retaliated for hostile shelling of BOESINGHE. Bad weather. Wet & stormy. Fired 10 rds at STEAM MILL B.6.d.3.3. and also 4.5 how at STEAM MILL B.6.d.3.3. suspected	
	29/12/16		M.G. at 5.30, 6.30, 6.30 & 7.30.	
	30/12/16		115th Infantry Bde relieved in the BOESINGHE sector by the 116th Infantry Bde, the 11th Battn. Sussex Regt in front line. Three bursts of retaliatory fire in morning for hostile shelling of our support line. Some registration with aeroplane observation. Two hits on a M.G. emplacement at STEAM MILL by 4.5 hows.	
	31/12/16		11 am – 12.30 pm registration by howitzers, who also fired 20 rds at suspected O.P. in CANON FARM C.1.C.5.3. Very mild, but weather still changeable.	

A. Smelley Wilmot —
Col.
Comdg. 179th Brigade. R.F.A.

WAR DIARY or INTELLIGENCE SUMMARY

Army Form C. 2118

179 Bde RFA
Vol XI

Place	Date	Hour	Summary of Events and Information	Remarks and references to Appendices
ELVERDINGHE	1/1/17	11 am to 4.15 pm	Several points & barrage lines registered. Considerable hostile minenwerfer activity on the left of our front & Belgians, about 3.35 – 4.15 pm. We retaliated heavily but fired 145 rds. before the enemy was silenced.	
	2/1/17		Chiefly registration.	
	3/1/17		Enemy minenwerfer engaged by B and D batteries and silenced. Belgians on our left during afternoon heavily shelled by hostile minenwerfer, called for retaliation from this group, 42 rounds fired by B battery which reduced enemy activity.	
	4/1/17		Major Bell, Captain Kickelly and Lieut Willoughby awarded Military Cross. More than usual activity on part of enemy artillery, B battery and occasionally A battery positions shelled from 1.0 to 4.0 pm with about 200, 5.9 and 4.2" no casualties and very little material damage done. Only one gun pit being hit, no damage to guns or ammunition.	
	5/1/17		Enemy activity confined to Minenwerfer. Our own artillery registered hostile minne work was going on in enemy lines	
	6/1/17		Hostile Minnie very active. 60th & 5" Howitzers and 18 pdr retaliated and enemy ceased shooting.	
	7/1/17		Hostile Trench Mortars active, retaliation called for by infantry and given by group artillery.	

Army Form C. 2118

WAR DIARY
or
INTELLIGENCE SUMMARY

(Erase heading not required.)

Instructions regarding War Diaries and Intelligence Summaries are contained in F. S. Regs., Part II. and the Staff Manual respectively. Title Pages will be prepared in manuscript.

Place	Date	Hour	Summary of Events and Information	Remarks and references to Appendices
SUERDINGE	8/1/17		Few 77 mm shells fired at BOESINGHE but beyond this rest of day very quiet.	
	9/1/17		Enemy 77 mm and T.M's active on Front Line. A battery retaliated on T.M's when shelling ceased.	
	10/1/17		A few 5.9 rounds put over onto A and B batteries, one day-out at A battery being hit, no damage to personnel, one pair of binoculars smashed. Enemy T.M. again active, retaliation given.	
	11/1/17		Very quiet day, no hostile shelling and no shelling by our own guns.	
	12/1/17		All batteries fired up D 25 rounds each on hostile 77 mm gun position at U.25.d.4.7. suspected of being the battery that had been shelling BOESINGHE during previous days.	
	13/1/17		Quiet day. Few hostile rounds at Front Line.	
	14/1/17		14 hostile rounds at Support Line beyond this nothing to report.	
	15/1/17		Nothing to report. Snow fell in the evening	

WAR DIARY
or
INTELLIGENCE SUMMARY
(Erase heading not required.)

Army Form C. 2118

Place	Date	Hour	Summary of Events and Information	Remarks and references to Appendices
ELVERDINGHE	1/1/17		Quiet day. Relief by section of A/179.	
	12/1/17		Finish of relief of A/179. Few enemy shells on BOESINGHE.	
	18/1/17		Brigade ceased to exist. A battery became A/277 Army Brigade	
			C/119 to D/174	
			B — — —	
			C Right section to D/186	
			C Left — to D/277	
			D Right — to D/119	
			D Left — to +DAC	
			J+Q absorbed by 39 +DAC.	

C.W. Loughlin
Adjutant, 179th Brigade, R.F.A.
for Col.
Commanding 170th Brigade, R.F.A.

[Stamp: 179 BRIGADE / 18 JAN 1917 / ROYAL FIELD ARTILLERY]

See 5 ARMY TROOPS

www.ingramcontent.com/pod-product-compliance
Lightning Source LLC
Chambersburg PA
CBHW081535160426
43191CB00011B/1764